EAST IN EDEN

EAST IN EDEN

William Niblo & His Pleasure Garden of Yore

BY

BENJAMIN FELDMAN

The Green-Wood Historic Fund
IN ASSOCIATION WITH
New York Wanderer Press
NEW YORK

COVER:

"Tommy" and friends with a New York City lady; Courtesy of The Collection of Tom Burnett.

FRONTISPIECE:

FIGURE 1: *Portrait of William Niblo in late middle age, artist unknown (but cf. Figure 3); Courtesy of Harvard Theatre Collection, Houghton Library, Harvard University.*

ISBN - 978-1-4951-1546-2

Copyright ©2014 Benjamin Feldman

CONTENTS

FOREWORD   7

CHAPTER 1:   *A Pensive Resort*   9
CHAPTER 2:   *A Legendary Larder*   15
CHAPTER 3:   *Eden On The Hudson*   27
CHAPTER 4:   *Disaster And Rebirth*   52
CHAPTER 5:   *Calvary Church*   72
CHAPTER 6:   *Niblo's Empire*   83
CHAPTER 7:   *A Dignified End*   91

EPILOGUE   97
INDEX   115

FOREWORD

Fingertip access to our favorite performers has long been a way of life in America—for so long, in fact, that we cannot imagine it otherwise. The talking machine age began with Edison in 1877. Before the Victrola and its forebears, and before radio, television, and the Internet existed, one could only hear popular performers if one lived in a town where touring artists stopped and played at the local opera hall. So attuned are we inhabitants of the twenty-first century to flipping a switch on an electronic device and surrounding ourselves easily and cheaply with all manner of aural and visual amusement that it is easy to forget what came before. Until the final quarter of the nineteenth century, sensory experience of live entertainment required a trip outside the home, with the exception of parlor sing-alongs and soirees in wealthy homes and royal courts. Nonprint media were unborn. Today, enjoying live artistic performance no longer requires planning ahead. Electronic consumption has altered our senses.

Live presentations of all manner of performing arts, and their venues, had a different importance in nineteenth-century New York than in later years. The reputation of the city's impresarios of the 1800s far outstripped that of the names, hardly boldface today, who retain control of Broadway and other stages and various concert halls. Ask a random, well-educated city-dweller the identities of the owners and operators of the most important houses in the Theater District, and one is likely to draw a blank stare. Shubert and Nederlander will ring a dim bell, though these families have been involved for more than a century on the Great White Way. Today, studios of all kinds, be they virtual or three-dimensional, surround us 24/7 with content on demand, their masters largely anonymous. In the late 1860s, quite the opposite obtained. Keene, Wallack, Christy, Palmo, Barnum, and Miner were all well known to a vast swath of mid- and late nineteenth-century New Yorkers as performers and impresarios of theater, opera, and various entertainments on a proscenium stage. Only Barnum's name survives today, but for decades another name outshone even the great Phineas T: William Niblo stood alone.

Though Niblo left precious few items of personal correspondence and was reluctant to have his photo taken (unlike virtually every other figure in the mid-nineteenth-century entertainment world), his mark on popular entertainment in New York City was enormous and his name known far and wide. Almost every day from the early 1820s until the end of 1894, Niblo's name appeared in print in many New York City daily newspapers, advertising his tavern and hostelry downtown (1813–28) and his pleasure garden (a genteel outdoor and indoor saloon, promenade, and proscenium theater), which was established on the northern reaches of settled Manhattan in 1828 and lasted until 1894. The content of those advertisements, be they menus or playbills, and the contemporary food and theater criticism, as well as the accounts, both private and published, of his contemporaries and customers, all paint a fascinating picture of a glorious part of New York's history, and America's too.

Chapter 1
A PENSIVE RESORT

Late one summer afternoon, a few years after the end of the Civil War, an elderly, balding gentleman passed through the brownstone gates of Brooklyn's vast Green-Wood Cemetery. Dressed inconspicuously, with a novel in hand, the old man headed to the southern quadrant of the several-hundred-acre burial grounds. A huge brass key weighed heavily in his hands, the match to a well-used padlock on a cast-iron mausoleum door on Crescent Avenue. It had been a long trip to South Brooklyn from the visitor's lodgings near Manhattan's Madison Square Park, and the gatekeepers nodded their customary greeting to the habitual guest. Only a few years before, he was world renowned. Despite his retirement from an illustrious career right after the fall of Fort Sumter, the name of William Niblo remained in common parlance throughout the entertainment world as well as with the public.

Fame and reputation had been Niblo's stock in trade for more than five decades. Anyone who would be or was well known ate and drank at Niblo's famed Bank Coffee House on Pine Street between 1813 and 1828: politicians, theater celebrities, and wannabes of every sort quaffed ales and stuffed themselves with game from Niblo's well-stocked larder. From 1828 onward, after the founding of Niblo's eponymous pleasure garden, his name became a household word across America and Europe. Visiting performers to the United States, the already famous as well as aspiring show-people, found their way to the proscenium stage of Niblo's Garden. The complex stood, in various incarnations, on a site on Broadway between Prince and Houston Streets, and lasted until 1894 under Niblo's name even though he retired from the operation in 1861.

During his 33-year tenure as owner/operator, all manner of shows were mounted in the largest auditorium. Opera, orchestral, and vocal music filled the hall, but more spectacular visual fare also abounded.

 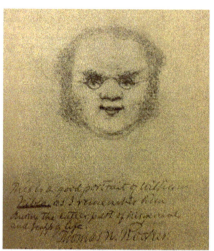

FIGURE 2: *Portrait of William Niblo in middle age, artist unknown, appearing in Col. Thomas Picton,* Old Gotham Theatricals *(San Bernardino, CA, Borgo Press, 1999), p. 21.*

FIGURE 3: *Portrait of William Niblo in late middle age by James Cooper; Courtesy of The New York Public Library Theater Collection.*

Indoors and out, balloonists, equestrian shows, and magicians' sorcery pleased throngs of genteel New Yorkers. Niblo's Garden provided a decent, family-friendly alternative to the lower-class venues on the Bowery and adjoining streets. His customers paid a bit more and avoided the usual theatergoers' experience of unescorted women in their midst on their evenings out.

Despite a thorough and necessary involvement in the public's mind as a purveyor of genteel pleasures, Niblo himself was quite modest in some ways. Abjuring physical vanity was one of these. In the New York studios of Matthew Brady, Napoleon Sarony, and many others, theatrical, political, military, and business celebrities were constantly photographed, and the images converted into collectible "cabinet cards" and cartes des visite. But none of Niblo was made.

There are only three surviving images of Niblo, none of them photographs. From these depictions, an early twentieth-century author imagined Niblo's personality as that of a "plain, sturdy old man, who considered the portraiture of the human face an intolerable vanity."[1] The last of the three portraits above (and perhaps the first was by the same artist) is a rough pencil sketch, done 18 years after Niblo's death, by his acquaintance James G. Cooper, a writer for the *New-York Daily Tribune*. It shows a cheerful and benevolent face, decorated with black-rimmed spectacles and a curl-rimmed balding pate. An unidentified artist executed the second portrait (above) somewhat somber and presumably more realistic, after Niblo's death. Both of the images are consistent with a man whose "shrewdness and firmness of will" were legendary in his time, all the while he was "constantly smiling, saying 'Bless You!' and distributing quarters to the street urchins on his way about town."[2]

Although he brought smiles and laughter to hundreds of thousands of patrons each year, William Niblo lived in sorrow during the last 27 years of his life, following the 1851 death of his wife of 32 years, Martha King Niblo. The ornate, many-drawered mausoleum he completed in 1854 holds her remains as well as those of his mother, her parents, and other relatives and acquaintances. Niblo was devastated by Martha's premature death, which probably resulted from stomach cancer. She had been his full partner not only at home but in his business ventures. Her obituary in the *New-York Daily Tribune* of February 13, 1851, described Martha as

> eminently distinguished, having been for many years a co-laborer with her husband in the management of his extensive undertaking.—His handsome country residence, near Hell-Gate, was erected, and the grounds laid out, under her superintendence. Nor did she lack the softer attributes of woman's nature. She was a hospitable hostess to her guests, a generous sympathizer to her friends, and a charitable helper to all who needed her assistance. She will be missed from a large circle of society.

The couple was generous to family and friends alike, and in the last months of her life, critically ill Martha had the solace of having her widowed mother, Catherine King, live with her and William at their residence in the 14th Ward.[3] After Martha's death, Niblo was said to visit his wife's final resting place virtually every day he was in New York, despite a long trip via surface transportation from Manhattan to the Brooklyn ferry, and then by carriage up the Gowanus Hills from the Brooklyn docks. The round trip must have taken no less than four hours.

Niblo frequently brought friends with him to enjoy Green-Wood's beauty and serenity, to picnic and recreate in a public space that rivaled

Manhattan's Central Park and Brooklyn's Prospect Park (both created years after Martha's death). On a particular summer day in the late 1860s, though, Niblo was alone, ready to spend a leisurely few hours resting and reading inside the cool shade of the mausoleum, hard by the edge of Crescent Water. Its massive door creaked open as the short, portly visitor turned the key in the lock. Left wide open, the doorway allowed ample daylight into the somber space to enable Niblo to relax and read.

He made himself comfortable and settled into his routine on a warm afternoon, turning away from everyday life to dwell both in his novel and memories of the life he had shared with Martha. Deeply distracted, the reader noticed nothing of a huge storm brewing outside. All of a sudden, a huge gust of wind came up and the iron door blew shut, locking Niblo in the giant, soundproof tomb.

Niblo remained a widower after Martha died until his death in 1878. Though he played an active role as warden and vestryman at Gramercy Park's Calvary Episcopal Church and maintained a close relationship with Mary Sylvester, his housekeeper, no one kept strict track of his whereabouts. Only after he failed to return to his lodgings that evening did friends become concerned.

The next day, however, when it became apparent that he had not slept in his own bed, "alarm seized the household," according to an article published in the Batavia, New York, *Daily Morning News* on August 30, 1878, a few years after the incident (and nine days after Niblo's death). Searchers were sent to "the clubs, the theatres, the places of public resort" that Niblo frequented, but came up empty-handed.

Decades of vetting and promoting experts in legerdemain and escape artists of the likes of Signor Antonio Blitz proved of little use when Niblo himself was center stage. He sat in the dark, shrieking for help after the tomb door clanged shut, but soon lapsed into a calm, philosophical consideration of his circumstances, feeling certain that his friends would seek him out.

Luckily, such was indeed the case, and when inquiry was made at the gatehouse, the keeper realized that Niblo had come in the previous day but had not been seen leaving. The temporary prisoner was found forthwith, in calm repose, none the worse for his Stygian sleepover.

Niblo's life seems to have been a quiet one in many respects: though his business career was packed with an ever-increasing stream of new enterprises and investments, his personal life was measured and calm. The solid partnership formed and maintained with his wife Martha as well as his devout participation in Episcopal affairs in New York City left a record of a man married and widowed with scarcely a blemish on his personal reputation, save one unfortunate incident in his premarital life that likely plagued him with guilt toward a woman he did not marry, as well as toward the one he did.

Though perhaps his beginnings in New York started above those of a Ragged Dick, William Niblo's rapid ascent to the pinnacle of respectable life in New York's mercantile society is a classic American story of piety and hard work paying off. That story begins on Wall Street, near Slote Lane.

FIGURE 4: *The Bank of New York, c. 1813; Frederick Philipse's mansion at 47 Pine Street stood nearby; Courtesy of The New York Public Library Digital Gallery.*

Chapter 2
A LEGENDARY LARDER

No passenger ship lists survive from the years during which Niblo emigrated from Ireland to the United States. Unfortunately, his exact date of arrival is unknown. His death certificate fixes his arrival as having occurred in 1806, at age 16, but another primary source attests to Niblo's arrival year as 1802.[4] There is no evidence that Niblo's father John ever came to America, but his mother Mary certainly did, as did his brothers John (c. 1785–1866) and Robert (c. 1784–1819). Whether any of them came with William is unknown.[5]

Not long off the boat, Niblo trod a well-worn path on his way upward in bustling postindependence New York. Ambitious and personable, Niblo was in his early twenties when he established the Bank Coffee House at Frederick Philipse's former residence at 47 Pine Street in 1813, after, according to some accounts, having first worked for his future father-in-law, David King.[6]

King operated a porter house on Wall Street and in Slote-lane (now Beaver Street) from 1800 until 1820.[7] King was politically connected enough to have been paid by the City's Common Council for catering a number of expensive banquets as well as for renting out rooms at his tavern for meetings of the grand jury.[8] Niblo married David and Catherine King's daughter, Martha, on December 15, 1819, in a service performed by the Reverend Phillip Melancthon Whelpley of the First Presbyterian Church in lower Manhattan at 10 Wall Street. William's mother and his in-laws were members of the congregation.[9] The structure in which William and Martha Niblo were married was the second church on the site, and burned down in the Great Fire of 1835 (along with most of lower Manhattan).[10]

Coffee houses were a long-standing institution in pre- and postcolonial Manhattan, functioning not only as places of refreshment but also as communal meeting places and hostelries. The establishments served food and alcoholic beverages as well as coffee. The Bank Coffee House joined a century-old custom dating back to 1696, when John Hutchins opened the King's Arms in a sizable house with a garden at Broadway and Cedar Streets, near where Trinity Church would be first sited two years later.[11] The New Coffee House, the Atlantic Garden, the Exchange, the Merchants, and the Tontine all competed for the trade of merchants, bankers, and other businessmen who swarmed lower Manhattan.

King joined Niblo in operating the Bank Coffee House, some years after Niblo ended his apprenticeship with King and struck out on his own in 1813.[12] The Bank Coffee House stood across the street from a used furniture store owned by the mother of one of Niblo's business colleagues, a lucky happenstance when business became brisk: in the early years, when customers crowded in unexpectedly to Niblo's table, he would borrow furniture from the old lady.[13]

Niblo's hail-fellow-well-met personality served him well as a restaurateur, and the Bank quickly developed a large following among businessmen, politicians, and the theater world in the years when the Park Theater brought actors and their fans to the area.[14] City Park, bounded on the east by Park Row (known today as City Hall Park), formed the epicenter of New York for rich and poor alike, as one of the few green spaces in

FIGURE 5: *Wall Street Presbyterian Church Street, New York City; Courtesy of The New York Public Library.*

FIGURE 6: *View of Wall Street, 1825 (looking east from Trinity Church); from Henry Collins Brown,* New York of To-day, *The Old Colony Press, New York: 1917, p. 24.*

FIGURE 7: *View of Wall Street looking west,* by Samuel Hollyer; Collection of The New-York Historical Society.

town open to the public. The Park Theater sat adjacent, and its audiences could easily patronize Niblo's establishment before or after a show.

Niblo's hostelry was described in one contemporary account as "a famous house for good living . . . resorted to by strangers and country merchants, more than by private families." Prices for lodging were not cheap: "one dollar and a half per day, seven dollars and a half per week, or three hundred dollars per year," perhaps because its "vicinity near the Exchange, Banks, and Public Offices, renders it convenient for men of business."[15]

The fare at the Bank Coffee House was legendary, even in its day. Niblo's skills as a provisioner were essential to his success, but haute cuisine it was not; early American tastes were simple. New Yorkers' appetites for fresh game were insatiable, and specimens from all over the Eastern Seaboard were brought to the Niblo establishment and stored in his famous larder until consumed.

"How well we remember this celebrated house," wrote the author of an unidentified newspaper article clipped in Henry Onderdonk, Jr.'s 1863 scrapbook decades later,

FIGURE 8: *View of Park Row. 1825; Collection of The New-York Historical Society.*

for we kept our office exactly opposite to it thirty-three years ago. Niblo is no chicken now, although he was a young man then, and had served a long apprenticeship with his father-in-law David King . . . Niblo was a great favorite with customers [of King's establishment], and when he opened the Bank Coffee-house all his old friends clocked [sic] around him, and the house became celebrated for its choice old wines and well stocked larder . . . sixty feet long, in which you might see the hind quarters of a premium ox, saddles of venison, hundreds of canvas-back ducks, and every variety of game that air and water produce.

Saturday, February 15, 1823, was a particularly auspicious day in the annals of postcolonial gourmands. At 3:00 p.m., Niblo's cook, called by his boss "Chief Officer of the Mouth," served up a multicourse banquet at "The Ordinary."[16] The menu boggles the mind and senses. As parts of the first course, three soups were offered: terrapin, oxtail, and "Hare soup, in the Scottish style." An exotic fourth choice was also available: a broth of "Green Turtle, made of Calf's Head, after the style of Osborne . . . while Grand Officer of the Mouth to Sir Joseph Banks and Sir William Curtis."[17] Trout from Carman's pond in Long Island were said to be "remarkably fine," but one might wonder when the season ended, prior to this mid-February banquet, and how the catch was stored.

Game dishes formed the second course on banquet day. A "Bald Eagle shot on the Grouse plains of Long Island: a very fine bird and very heavy" shared the bill of fare with a "remarkably fine Hawk and Owl, shot in Turtle Grove, Hoboken," and an "extraordinary fine opossum, taken at Plank ridge, Virginia." Rounding out the selections was some "remarkably fine Bear meat. The bear was despatched at the Big Bone (Lick) in Kentucky," and served with a "Raccoon, killed in Communipau [sic; New Jersey]," which was "flayed and to be seen hanging in the larder" prior to the banquet.[18] Last but not least among the choices was a "Wild Swan, most wonderful in size, six feet and eleven inches from the tip of the tail to the point of the beak, and nine feet eleven inches from the extremity of each wing. It was called at Havre de Grace [Maryland] a mighty fine bird and very heavy." One also could speculate about the methods, if any, of refrigeration employed for the game brought from afar. It was several days' journey to New York from Havre de Grace, and even further from Big Bone Lick, Kentucky, via rutted wagon roads. Winter temperatures had their advantages, despite making the journey more difficult in most ways.

As if the first two courses were not enough to satiate a lumberjack, on came a third, "served up with substantials, such as a saddle of very fine Venison, weighing nearly eighty pounds, killed in Chenango county [New York], a saddle of Albany mutton which took the premium two years ago, two wild Turkeys, shot in the backwoods of Pennsylvania," roasted beef from Dutchess County (New York) canvass-back ducks from Lazaretto, Pennsylvania,[19] "16 pounds per pair," partridges and quail beyond number, "Reindeer and Buffalo Tongues from Russia, Hares Roasted and Ragout of Hares, Hams from Westphalia, Venison Pasty, Kebobbed Mutton, Stewed Macaroni, Oyster and Quail Pies and Smoked Geese and Trout." The third course also offered "Snapping turtle, Calipash and Calipee Terrapins from [the] James River, dressed in the southern mode."

Puddings, pies, tarts, jellies, and fruits made up the dessert course at a price of fifty cents each, to be consumed with a selection of wines that included Rickett's Old Madeira at $3 a bottle, warranted by the tavernkeep to be 27 years old. For the same tariff, one could sip "Boston Wine," only one year younger, the "Stackpole and Denny Wines" of similar price and vintage, and "East India wine," said to have aged five years in wood and twelve in the bottle, at a slightly lower price. Many other vintages from the London docks were made available, and perhaps a good bit of drinking was in order to wash down all those dainties.

Henry Onderdonk, author of the above reminiscences, looked on with amazement that winter's day "to see the connoisseurs drop in by pairs and singly." Decorum at American taverns was *sui generis:*

> Ten minutes before the hour appointed, the word was given; "Clear the passage! Here comes the bear!" And sure enough, a huge bear, smoking hot, was served up whole, standing on its two hind legs. Next came the buck with tail standing erect—for in those days buck tails stood high, and were plenty. Everything being served, the dinner was announced, but there was not half room enough for the company, so side tables were spread in the halls in every direction.

Exclamations filled the halls as diners competed for the attention of harried waiters and the choicest slices of venison and owl. Whether any leftovers remained at the end of the afternoon, much less how long the festivities lasted, remains unknown.

Though Niblo maintained a reputation as a gentle and welcoming tavernkeep, he was not above using the threat of physical violence as well as its occasional execution to keep order in his premises and to discipline employees. A contemporary observer who described the proprietor as

FIGURE 9: *The Corner of Pine Street and Broadway, 1820, by Samuel Hollyer; Collection of The New-York Historical Society.*

"naturally gentle and [as] kind-hearted as a girl, [who] showed the spirit of the man when aroused," recalled Niblo brandishing a red-hot fire poker at a group of ten British military officers who violated their promise to observe American sabbath customs during a Sunday dinner.[20] Niblo was sued unsuccessfully in 1817 by a woman named Ann Furey for having assaulted her, but lost two cases brought in 1819 and 1820 by an allegedly drunken cook, Michael Flood, who charged Niblo with unpaid wages and assault.[21] The proprietor also had several run-ins with municipal authorities over alleged infractions of various city ordinances, among them a privy constituting a nuisance (1817 and 1824), violation of fire codes in the construction of a two-story addition to the building (1818), permitting gambling in the tavern (1821), the unlawful keeping of a billiard table in the premises (1822), and failure to pay a municipal assessment for the widening of William Street, which was part of Niblo's responsibilities as lessee of the former Philipse mansion.[22]

After almost a decade of prosperity on Pine Street, Niblo decided to expand his franchise north and west of the civic center. In the early decades of the nineteenth century, throngs of New Yorkers with the means to do so fled uptown in the summertime to avoid the periodic outbreaks of deadly yellow fever. Greenwich Village was then a separate community, and its site on the banks of the Hudson River was deemed more salubrious than the crowded, pestilential streets downtown. By the early 1820s, Greenwich, as it was then known, had developed a separate commercial center with hastily erected structures. A contemporary journalist observed the completion of Niblo's second Bank Coffee House over a three-day period in August 1822 at the corner of Asylum (now West 4th) and Perry Streets, where corn had grown three days before.[23] Niblo advertised his Greenwich enterprise as early as August 30 that year in the *New-York Evening Post*, touting its proximity to the local custom house, post office, and banks, as well as his menu, to local merchants, residents, and travelers alike.

The second Bank Coffee House was only one project in a growing Niblo empire. In partnership with his brother John, Niblo operated a sizable hotel at the corner of Broadway and Cedar Streets across from Trinity Churchyard, and began provisioning public events. These undertakings included renting a house to sell refreshments hard by the Union

Course (near 75th Street in present-day Woodhaven, Queens). On May 27, 1823, a crowd of 50,000 (including the then-governor of Florida, Andrew Jackson) assembled to witness a race won by American Eclipse (representing the Northern states) against Sir Henry (for the South). Niblo even hired special messengers to relay news of the winner to his downtown Bank Coffee House, where the results were posted for all to see.

FIGURE 10: *American Eclipse, by Edward Troye.*

Niblo frequently turned to the daily newspapers to publicize the latest offerings on his tables. On January 4, 1825, the *New-York Evening Post* reported:

> Canvass-Back Ducks: A Fresh arrival of those delicious birds just arrived at the Bank Coffee House, to begin the New Year with. Rooms always in readiness and comfortably warm. The Coffee room is well supplied with game of every description: beef venison, steaks and chops, terrapin and oyster soups; broths; relishes &c.

The following August 1, the *Post* announced the arrival of "70 prime Green Turtles" for Niblo's tables. They were "kept healthy and fresh in the crawl at the foot of Warren St. Parties and Clubs accommodated with Turtle and Game dinners in the very first style. Soup of a delicious flavor ready every day at 11 o'clock. Mutton and gravy soups at the same hour." Niblo's turtle soup volume was huge: he also rented space for a live turtle storage crib in a slip at the foot of Clark Street in Brooklyn Heights from Henry Waring, and paid his rent with a fine specimen once a year.[24]

Green turtles were enormously popular in early nineteenth-century America as well as England. Though the stocks, mainly from the South Seas, would be depleted well before mid-century, substitutions were made, whether of Chesapeake Bay terrapin or other "mock-turtle" fare. A social club was even formed for the stated purpose of consuming the favored flesh. *The National Advocate* reported on August 3, 1819, that the members of the Hoboken Turtle Club were "commanded to attend at Turtle Place ... to perform spoon exercise."[25]

Even before he opened his second Bank Coffee House, Niblo found promise in many other ventures. Legitimate and genteel pleasure resorts that relied on day-trippers for their custom particularly interested him. On May 31, 1817, an advertisement and news article in the *New-York Evening Post* announced his establishment of the "Marine Baths," a set of enclosed basins set in the North (now Hudson) River at the Battery. In an era when bathrooms were unknown, and truly clean water in sufficient quantity for bathing was unavailable, the Marine Baths offered a valuable choice. Both cold and warm baths plus "refreshments of every description" were offered to men, ladies, and families, in the public enclosure as well as in private ones. The ability of the proprietor to raise the basins entirely out of the North River was touted as a means of ensuring maximum cleanliness. According to one memoirist, these Marine Baths were the first public baths in Manhattan, but in fact Niblo seems to have taken over the location and perhaps even the physical facilities of an operation started as early as 1814 by Willis Merritt.[26]

Four years later, another venture blossomed on what is now the Upper East Side of Manhattan. On the river side of what is now First Avenue, between 60th and 62nd Streets, a large mansion and carriage house had been built at the end of the eighteenth century and briefly occupied by the family of Abigail Adams Smith. The property included a "blood horse" race and trotting course, and luxuriant gardens suitable for "running, pitching the quoit, and other gymnastic enterprises." Niblo acquired

MARINE BATH.

WILLIAM NIBLO respectfully informs the public, the New-York Marine Bath is now open for the reception of company at Mr. *James Arden's Wharf*, near the *Battery*, in the North River.—No pains or expense has been spared to make this establishment as complete as possible—An entrance, is making from the street, so that ladies can walk down the wharf without any inconvenience. The large or public bath is exceedingly spacious, and the private baths very numerous and convenient. There is also *two Shower Baths*, one in the Ladies' and the other in the Gentlemen's apartments.—The Bath is constructed upon a buoyant principle, and supplied with pumps and other machinery to raise the whole bath out of the water, for the purpose of cleaning the same, and also for accommodating the depth of water to the liking of the bathers.

The situation chosen for the bath is far superior to any other on account of the purity of the water; and when the utility of an establishment, so conducive to health and pleasure, is properly considered, he flatters himself he will receive the encouragement of the heads of families, and others.

A proper person is appointed to the management of the bath, and no pains will be spared to give satisfaction to the ladies and gentlemen who are pleased to visit the establishment.

TERMS.

Families for the season,		$7 00
Single person	do.	4 00
Single bath		00 25
Or, 6 baths for		1 00

Shower baths, a separate charge.

Subscriptions received at the Bath, or at the Bank Coffee-House.

Refreshments of every description necessary for such an establishment, will always be kept, and the greatest care will be taken in procuring proper attendants

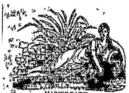

FIGURE 11: *Advertisement for Niblo's Marine Baths;* New York Evening Post *May 31, 1817.*

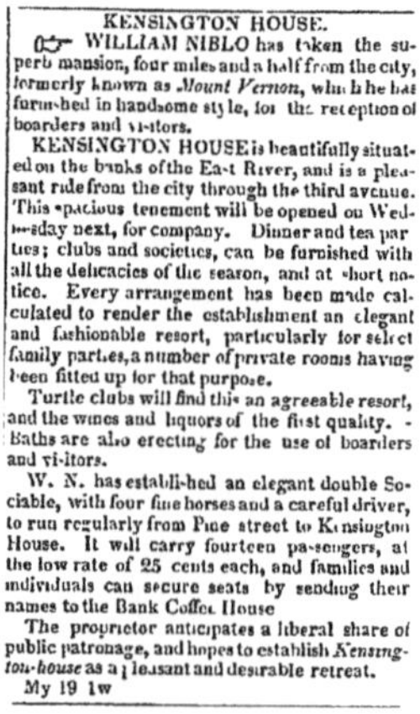

KENSINGTON HOUSE.

WILLIAM NIBLO has taken the superb mansion, four miles and a half from the city, formerly known as *Mount Vernon*, which he has furnished in handsome style, for the reception of boarders and visitors.

KENSINGTON HOUSE is beautifully situated on the banks of the East River, and is a pleasant ride from the city through the third avenue. This spacious tenement will be opened on Wednesday next, for company. Dinner and tea parties; clubs and societies, can be furnished with all the delicacies of the season, and at short notice. Every arrangement has been made calculated to render the establishment an elegant and fashionable resort, particularly for select family parties, a number of private rooms having been fitted up for that purpose.

Turtle clubs will find this an agreeable resort, and the wines and liquors of the first quality.—Baths are also erecting for the use of boarders and visitors.

W. N. has established an elegant double Sociable, with four fine horses and a careful driver, to run regularly from Pine street to Kensington House. It will carry fourteen passengers, at the low rate of 25 cents each, and families and individuals can secure seats by sending their names to the Bank Coffee House

The proprietor anticipates a liberal share of public patronage, and hopes to establish *Kensington-house* as a pleasant and desirable retreat.

My 19 1w

FIGURE 12: *Advertisement for Kensington House;* The Evening Post *[New York] May 21, 1821.*

control of the property during the summer of 1821, renaming it the Kensington House.[27] A magnificent coach, seating twenty and led by a team of six fine gray steeds, ferried customers from the Bank Coffee House to Niblo's first essay at an outdoor pleasure garden, in the fashion of late eighteenth-century London establishments at Vauxhall and Ranelagh. "Kensington Gardens" sat on a large plot along the banks of the East River near present-day 61st Street, with a splendid house in its midst. "The Sociable," as Niblo called his equipage, was driven by a celebrated coachman, Bill Black, dressed in white coat and hat, white top boots, and white gloves. Luxury and plenty were Niblo's trademarks, and he spared no expense in fashioning a memorable experience for his customers at Kensington. Horticultural fairs and cattle shows were conducted there, and genteel customers could partake of the river breezes, sipping sherry and spooning sorbets, far away from the filth and clatter of lower Manhattan's crowded and unhealthy streets.

The venture was not profitable, though. Scarcely a month after Niblo had reannounced the establishment in February 1822 (presumably for visitors during the coming warmer months), an advertisement appeared in the *New-York Evening Post* announcing a new operator of the establishment. On March 27, 1822, Niblo advertised the sale of "The Sociable," and presumably ceased operation of the Kensington House.

The mansion burned down in 1826; only the carriage house survived. That structure, built in 1799, operated as the Mount Vernon

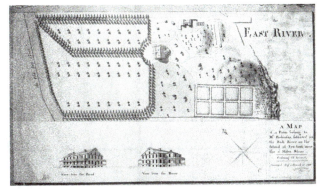

FIGURE 13: *Map of Grounds of The Mount Vernon Hotel (1806): The stables and carriage house are shown in the top center of the image; Collection of The New-York Historical Society.*

Hotel from 1826 until 1833. It survives today as a museum operated by the Colonial Dames of America.

Less than one year after his sale of "The Sociable," Niblo embarked on another hostelry, far from town. The August 24, 1822, issue of the *New-York Evening Post* announced his acquisition of a "large and elegant House on the Third Ave.," which he intended to fit up "for his Boarders." A coach would run back and forth to the second Bank Coffee House, then under construction, and Niblo also offered in the advertisement to erect a separate "Exchange" for his merchant hostelry customers if they so desired.

With his eye on larger prizes, Niblo gave up the original Bank Coffee House in 1828, selling out to James Fossett and David Earle, who moved the operation to 39 Pine Street. Uptown, Niblo found much larger fish to fry.

FIGURE 14: *The Mount Vernon Hotel today; author photo.*

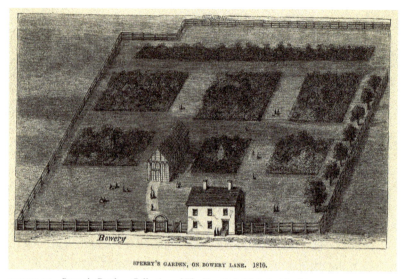

FIGURE 15: *Sperry's Garden; Collection of The New-York Historical Society.*

Chapter 3
EDEN ON THE HUDSON

Despite the mixed successes of his enterprises other than the Bank Coffee House, Niblo fastened upon yet another opportunity to expand his entertainment and hostelry empire in 1827, when a portion of the colonial-era Bayard Farm became available. The parcel, located on the northeast corner of Houston and Prince Streets, had been devoted to a circus and equestrian facility in the earlier years of the nineteenth century. According to one account, even before the circus use, Alderman Charles Henry Hall had occupied one of the houses on the site and constructed an elaborate ornamental stable for his favorite race horses:

> [A]long the entire rear of the garden, fronting upon Crosby Street, ran a shingle palace, a marvelous structure of wood and glass, divided into chambers, the entrance to which bore the name of its equine tenant in huge golden letters, so that all the world might know that Whalebone or some other high-mettled racer dwelt therein in dignity and clover.[28]

The property ended up as a public equestrian facility. Known for some years as "The Stadium," the parcel, far from the center of populated New York, was purchased by Stephen Van Rensselaer III for $15,000 and used as a drill ground for militia after the outbreak of the War of 1812.[29] Renamed Columbian Gardens by a new operator, in 1823 it saw performances by acrobats, musicians, and singers during the summer. A tavern named the Sans Souci operated in one of the two houses on the Broadway frontage in the years before Niblo took control of the block. Niblo continued to take paying overnight guests in the houses even as his new enterprise opened for business, resolving to turn the outdoor grounds into an ornamental pleasure garden.[30]

Pleasure gardens first appeared in New York near the end of the eighteenth century, modeled in a modest way after their ornate predecessors in London. The earliest British version, Spring Gardens, comprised eleven acres carved out of the northeast corner of St. James Park during the reign of James I. A bathing pool and bowling green were available to visitors, as well as expensive refreshments. The establishment moved to the Vauxhall neighborhood in 1661 and remained there until, under its second name, Vauxhall Gardens finally closed in 1859.

Seventeenth-century pleasure gardens in London included Hampstead Wells, Sadler's Wells, and Marylebone Gardens. Putatively "fresh" water was available in the "wells" of some of these establishments, flowing from natural springs on-site and plumbed into bathing pools in private enclosures. Twenty others opened in London during the eighteenth century, including the magnificent Ranelagh Gardens and the Bermondsey Spa. Pleasure gardens tried to limit admission to genteel ladies and gentlemen, charging a significant admission fee to visitors to stroll the lushly planted grounds and partake of sherbets, iced teas, and punches in outdoor and indoor saloons. Live performances were offered in amphitheaters and enclosed proscenium stages, and middle-class citizens could enjoy a taste of the life of estate owners in the countryside. By the middle of the nineteenth century, though, these elaborate places of recreation had virtually disappeared from London, due to the pressure of real estate development and the burgeoning metropolitan population.[31]

The same fashions dictated the development of Niblo's Garden at a site that was, in the late 1820s, an exurban location. As early as 1750, a resort near Warren and Greenwich Streets named Bowling Green Garden changed its name to Vauxhall, in frank imitation of its London predecessor. Five others were so named in Manhattan, including three constructed and operated by Frenchman Joseph Delacroix. His last "Vauxhall" was developed on a site between Broadway and the Bowery, between Great Jones and Eighth Streets.[32] Another account states that Jacob Sperry, a Swiss emigrant to New York, acquired a property where Vauxhall was ultimately established and, after using it for his florist and horticulture business, sold it to John Jacob Astor in 1803. Astor then leased the site to Delacroix for 21 years. Above is an 1810 image of "Sperry's Garden." Perhaps some knew the property under its prior owner's name, even though "Vauxhall" was well known by that time. All manner of genteel performances occurred there, ballet being realized by females in "properly lengthened skirts."[33]

Within a few years after New York's Eighth Street Vauxhall opened, aeronauts were delighting crowds there, ascending in elegantly decorated balloons as much as 36 feet in circumference. These shows were an enormously popular attraction both at Vauxhall and at Niblo's and their competitors in the late 'teens and thereafter.[34]

Many other pleasure gardens operated during the early years of New York's Vauxhall, among them the Columbian Garden on State Street opposite the Battery (perhaps a predecessor to one with a similar name that according to some accounts occupied the site of Niblo's Garden in 1823). The Union Garden was at Broadway and Cedar Streets, the United States Garden a few blocks north, and the Washington Gardens at Spring and Hudson Streets in Greenwich.

Elaborate fireworks displays depicting historical and biblical scenes as well as patriotic icons realized in blazing colors were tremendously popular among pleasure garden patrons. According to contemporary journalist Col. Thomas Picton, "Pyrotechnical exhibitions in those primitive days of sight-seeing were the popular rage and no outdoor assemblage, political or social, could disperse without a volley of detonations or a burst of rose-tinted flame."[35]

A typical fireworks display at Vauxhall was announced in the *New-York Evening Post* on May 26, 1808:

> Grand Pieces: 1. The Caducus [sic] of Mercury. 2. The Vertical Wheels called the Roly Polys, in pursuit of each other, on a horizontal platform. 3. A Girandole, forming a Vase, a White Circle, a Crown, and a Bouquet. 4. A Fixed five pointed Star in brilliant fire. 5. The Mosaic Rose Wheel, thirty six charges of fire. 6. The Ladies Caprice, with continual charges . . . 12. A combat of two Suns (first time) . . . 16. The admired piece of Mechanism called the fascination of the Rattle Snake—representing a serpent Fourteen feet long in pursuit of a butterfly . . .

Yet another fireworks display for June 24, 1808, was described in that evening's *Post*, including a "Masonic Pyramid, Bee-hive . . . Cross of Malta . . ." and the "Brilliant Portico of The Temple of Solomon, thirteen feet high and twenty-five feet in width with a large fixed Sun, Stars and other Masonic emblems. Admittance 4s—Doors open at six o'clock." The early arrivals at Vauxhall would have had plenty of time to walk the grounds and partake of the refreshments before darkness fell that summer day.[36]

Niblo used whatever advantages he could muster in his plans to create a demand for his new recreational venue. Though the area was not densely developed at the time, Niblo had at least two well-known neighbors in the immediate vicinity, houses of the writer James Fenimore Cooper, and the millionaire fur trader and merchant John Jacob Astor.[37]

Once Niblo gained control of the site, work proceeded rapidly. The stable was jacked up and moved so as to divide the garden into two parts, one of them providing a stage door onto Crosby Street for the building, repurposed as part of a theater. The ornamental dome was altered and an army of carpenters, scenic artists, and mechanics added pillars and galleries to create a 1,200-seat theater with a stage, a parquet, and two circles of boxes in just fifteen days. The structure continued the name Sans Souci, not only maintaining the goodwill of the previous use at the site, but also attempting to evoke some of the grandeur of the famous summer palace erected by Frederick the Great in Potsdam in the mid-eighteenth century.[38]

The notion of *rus in urbe* (an illusion of countryside in the city, according to a contemporary commentator) was central to Niblo's original creation. America, and New York in particular in the early nineteenth century, was considered the "new Eden," and the noise and filth that encroached everywhere in the developing metropolis threatened that conception. Pleasure gardens helped preserve the prevalent fantasy.[39]

Niblo invested heavily in rural and agricultural illusions, displaying exotic flowers, showcasing his gardens through illumination, and hosting the New York Horticultural Society's balls. Seating accommodations to partake of refreshments were at first somewhat primitive, designed to enhance the "rustic" nature of the venue. The market's demand for larger enclosed performance spaces in later years necessitated the construction of new structures on the site that attenuated the central garden-like atmosphere so important to Niblo's early success.[40] In the earliest years, a number of latticed boxes ringed a tall wooden structure, supplied with plain board seats with a rough table in the center, the whole encrusted with creeping vines. The refreshments included "a general collection of savory creams, fragrant teas, iced-lemonade, frosted-cakes, fruit-pies and such like dainties," as well as "iced-creams and punches, brandy peaches, wine sangarees, tongue sandwiches, and other condiments and beverages of a volatile nature." These were served "by a battalion of ebony-colored waiters in pure white aprons and baldrics of blue ribbon."[41]

In its early years, the garden was divided into north and south sections. The northerly one was decorated with cape jasmine, orange, lemon, and flowering magnolia trees. The southerly had a grand walk, adorned with illuminated arches supported by 24 illuminated lyres entwined with wreaths of flowers, as well as vases of brilliantly colored blossoms that supported colorful cut-glass globes, lighted with "oil gas" manufactured on premises. Thousands of variegated lamps and Chinese lanterns shone in the imported trees, and a mirror of more than three hundred square feet seemed to double the size of the walk. Other decorations included a hermit's cave, and a marine cavern glittering with stalactites and opening on a view of the sea. Niblo was a devoted patron of graphic arts, and hired well-known scenic artists of the day to decorate the space.[42]

The Sans Souci theater opened on Independence Day, 1828, with a magnificent program planned for the entire day. Banners were hung outside the garden at 4:00 a.m. advertising the day's festivities. A series of balloons were sent aloft, the first at noon, named after the glorious day, and others at one-hour intervals in honor of Washington, Jefferson, and Governor DeWitt Clinton. Madame Hannah Johnson, the first female balloonist in America, was scheduled to ascend at 4:00 p.m. At 6:00 p.m., theater impresario Charles Gilfert's players took the stage, presenting *The Hundred Pound Note* in a program that also included a tightrope performance by Herr Cline and various *pas de trois* by a group of French dancers. Still later in the evening, a final balloon, named in honor of soon-to-be President Andrew Jackson, was supposed to be launched, festooned with fireworks. It is unclear whether the ascent took place, as the next day one New York newspaper announced that the Sans Souci would be closed until July 9 for unspecified reasons. Apparently, a small fire had occurred.

Offerings continued throughout the summer months, and on August 7, the grounds were decorated with several thousand lamps and two faux temples erected. The ambience was second, in the opinion of a commentator, only to London's Vauxhall. Though the nights grew chilly and the theater ceased operations at the end of the summer, fireworks displays continued until October 14.[43]

By 1829, the Sans Souci was converted to "Niblo's Saloon," opening on Monday, May 18. The author of the premiere's program, a "New York Musical Festival" featuring the popular singer Charles King, recalled the first night as including portions of Handel's Messiah, presented with many notables in the house, including Stephen Van Rensselaer, former Mayor Philip Hone, John Jacob Astor, and John Delafield.

Within weeks of the conversion of the Sans Souci to a concert saloon, Niblo erected a larger theater on the commodious site. The stage was grand: 75 feet wide, 44 feet high, and 67 feet deep. The admission prices in 1830 were 75 cents for a single gentleman and $1 for a man and woman together. The ticket cost alone (in addition to the house policy) discouraged unaccompanied females from patronizing the establishment, and the rowdy crowds of whore-mongering men and so-called "sporting gentlemen" avoided Niblo's place. Only Niblo and Joseph Delacroix (among the dozens of pleasure garden operators) were consistently praised in the contemporary press for their ability to exclude prostitutes from their grounds. In various forms, the venue would be known as Niblo's Garden for six and a half decades, despite the continual shrinking of the outdoor garden as the indoor performance spaces were expanded and rebuilt.

Much of the advertising for New York's pleasure gardens emphasized the polite nature of the entertainment and reassured potential customers that the venue in question was respectable, elegant, and in the case of Niblo's, the "resort of the bon ton."[44] Niblo actively encouraged genteel women and families to participate in the various activities at his garden, inviting flower displays from female customers in 1839, and establishing family admission prices. Given his location quite some distance north of most pleasure gardens in New York, Niblo attempted to cater to upper-middle-class men and women who sought to retreat into their own private spaces and distance themselves from middle-brow consumers. Niblo's efforts in the early years were solidly aimed at the carriage trade. High admission fees, high-brow entertainment, and expensive refreshments helped accomplish his goal.[45] His efforts were not wholly successful, though, and the development of the city up to his doors, coupled with the gradual decrease in outdoor space at his garden and eventual redevelopment into a hotel and opera house complex, dictated the longevity of Niblo's Garden as a decidedly middle-of-the-road venue.[46]

Controlling both the nature of his patronage and the content offered on stage were key to the development of Niblo's goodwill and reliability as a provider of genteel entertainment. A piquant description of his business model was offered by contemporary journalist George Foster: "The secret of it is very simple—no woman is admitted at this house, under any pretext, unless accompanied by a gentleman. The consequence is that rowdies avoid the house, or, if they visit, have no inducement for misbehaving.—and respectable and quiet people come, with their wives and children, sure of being neither shocked by obscenity nor frightened by violence . . ."[47]

Thomas Goodwin, another contemporary in the musical performance world of Niblo's time, often spoke of his experiences at Niblo's Garden in its early years to his friend R. Osgood Mason, who recalled and published Goodwin's recollections many years later:

> [The so-called] Summer Theatre was a large, plain sort of building, fronting on Broadway, above the two residences already mentioned [Niblo's and James Fenimore Cooper's] and extending well back toward Crosby Street. It was, for those times, elaborately fitted up with mirrors and colored lights, and ornamented with pots of flowers and ferns. It at once became the fashionable place of amusement, and the garden, as a fresh breathing-place, with its shrubbery, flowers, arbors, and ice-cream long remained a great attraction.
>
> The bar and lunch-counters were together in a separate building opening both toward the theatre and toward the garden. The times of old-fashioned hospital-

FIGURE 16: *Niblo's Garden entrance on Broadway c. 1828; Courtesy of The New York Public Library Digital Images Collections.*

ity had not yet quite passed away, and on many an evening, or after some fatiguing rehearsal, a few members of the band or favorites of the company would find a comforting snack awaiting them. Old Dimulda, the wine-merchant was frequently on hand. "Why bless my soul!" the old man would say, in his foreign way, "I had altogether forgotten it, but it is my birthday; bring me half a dozen wine." And his birthday not uncommonly occurred two or three times a week.[48]

Niblo's programming, even in its earliest years, represented the evolution of New York's pleasure gardens from their predominantly tranquil, garden-like spaces to scenes of passive entertainment for their customers. Colonial-era pleasure gardens in New York changed with changing tastes: by the 1820s, customers desired performances, not just grounds upon which to stroll and sit and consume refreshments. Pleasure gardens destroyed their own essential character in the process while morphing into vitally important venues for opera, acrobatics, dramatic presentations of all kinds, and even sacred music.[49]

Patriotic presentations were important from day one. Niblo one-upped his competitor after Castle Garden presented "The Siege of Tripoli" to a crowd spellbound by a sea of green canvas and lurid light. In Castle Garden's show, the United States warship *Philadelphia* was blown up before their very eyes with the gallant Stephen Decatur in command of the disguised *Intrepid*, boarding the disabled Philadelphia and setting fire to it to deny the enemy its use in the First Barbary War. Profiting from the also quite recent Belgian revolution of 1830-1, Niblo presented "The Bombardment of Antwerp" with "a moving panorama of toy ships and wooden armies, extending from Broadway to Crosby Street, with bombs, skyrockets and cannonading enough to have thrown down the walls of Jerico [sic]."[50] New Yorkers were delighted, and Niblo's star rose high in the sky.

Though Niblo's was not the first pleasure garden in postcolonial New York, it was certainly one of the most lavish. As the outdoor space in Delacroix's final Vauxhall Garden decreased in size, it became déclassé, and Niblo's establishment benefited when Vauxhall's upper middle-class customers decamped.[51] Niblo's "surpassed all others in elegance and respectability, its status sustained by high entrance fees, expensive food, and urbane entertainments."[52] Its only competitor for posh patronage was Contoit's New York Garden on Broadway between Leonard and

Franklin Streets, a cozy and quiet resort for wealthy and well-bred ladies and unchaperoned genteel couples. Niblo's waiters, dressed in white jackets and aprons, dispensed lemonade, pound cake, and vanilla, lemon, or strawberry ice cream of a Sunday afternoon, and from sundown to midnight Niblo's was illuminated by colored whale-oil lamps on stanchions and branches of trees.[53]

FIGURE 17: *Coach from Niblo's Garden fleet, 1829:* Charles Haynes Haswell, Memoirs of an octogenarian of the City of New York (1816-1860) *(New York: Harper and Brothers, 1896), p. 238.*

Things did not always run smoothly at Niblo's, however. Only 19 days after participating in the opening-day program at the new venue, Madame Hannah Johnson was scheduled to go aloft again in her balloon rig, but when 20,000 spectators showed up and her ascent was canceled because of problems with the gas generator, a near-riot ensued. Madame Johnson sent the balloon aloft with no one aboard, and unruly, disgruntled, unticketed spectators tried to force their way into Niblo's Garden, injuring several policemen in the melee.[54] Johnson sued Niblo in early September in the Court of Common Pleas, claiming that Niblo had defaulted on paying her the $300 she alleged was due. Her claim was not upheld, and she was forced to pay Niblo's court costs.[55] Thirteen years later at Niblo's, a wealthy Southern planter stabbed and seriously wounded a Brazilian diplomatic attaché whom the assailant deemed to be trifling with the southerner's wife's affections.[56]

Lack of public transportation to the exurban site of Niblo's Garden might have posed a problem to a less resourceful entrepreneur. In the day, Broadway stages refrained from traveling north beyond the Broadway House hostelry at Grand Street. Even getting to Grand Street (far uptown from the center of New York in the late 1820s) could be a challenge. According to one contemporary observer, fewer than eighty hacks were available in the city, and perhaps a dozen families owned private carriages of any size. Niblo's fashionable patrons from the environs of Bowling

35

FIGURE 18: *Broadway, Looking North from Canal Street to Beyond Niblo's Garden: 1836; Courtesy of New York Public Library Digital Images Collection.*

Green and City Hall who lacked their own equipage were forced to hire a hack or debark from the public stagecoach at Grand Street and tramp northward on the muddy street. In characteristic fashion, Niblo turned a negative into a profitable positive by commissioning the construction in London of a fleet of special chocolate-colored stagecoaches with flat, patented springs and low bodies. The coaches, with Niblo's name illuminated on signboards affixed to the passenger compartments, were imported and driven by "tip-top whips, four in hand" on a route between the old Washington Hotel opposite Bowling Green and Niblo's new establishment. Some of the stages likely stopped at the Congress Hall Hotel, run by William's brother, John, at 112 Broadway, as well as other convenient places. The fare was one shilling (12½ cents). Niblo turned public benefactor with his transportation initiative, and ultimately sold off the stage line at a profit.[57]

Property records from 1832 describe the furnishings acquired by the optimistic entrepreneur in a transaction with New York fur trader and merchant Ramsay Crooks. Crooks turned over control of the "Houses No. 576 and 578 Broadway" to Niblo in November 1832, together with an inventory of luxurious household furniture recorded on four pages in the New York City Register's Office. "Marseilles," "Ingram" and "Brus-

FIGURE 19: *The Departure of the Israelites From Egypt – copy done by H. Sebron after original burned at Niblo's in 1835.*

sels" carpets, numerous feather beds, an "Astral Lamp," mahogany furniture, and an assortment of bric-a-brac fill the ledger pages, followed by details of hundreds of shrubs, trees, and other ornamental plants decorating the grounds.[58] Lemon, orange, citron, and "Malabar Nut" trees, a "large Century Aloe," eighty rose bushes, and dozens of geraniums of several species were purchased by Niblo. The total value of the plantings came to just under $2,000.

Niblo even petitioned the Board of Aldermen in 1835 to be allowed to plumb a water line from the system of pipes in Broadway for the purpose of drawing hundreds of gallons per night to operate an ornamental fountain in his Garden. His request was denied, though, when members of the Common Council objected to the potential diminution of flow available to fight fires in the rest of the city.[59] Within twelve months, Niblo would have good reason to greatly regret their decision.

With his control of the entire site, Niblo now had the freedom to introduce novel forms of public entertainment that had come into vogue in Europe in the late eighteenth and early nineteenth century. By the end of 1834, he erected a large brick building that fronted on Broadway (adjacent to #578) and imported huge paintings from London, including David Roberts's "The Departure of the Israelites from Egypt."

Londoners had enjoyed panoramic presentations since 1781. The Eidophusikon was an invention of Drury Lane scenic designer Philippe de Loutherbourg, rigged up in a small proscenium theater behind Leicester Square in which audiences were treated to static landscape and epic views. De Loutherbourg's success led, twelve years later, to the invention of the Panorama by Robert Barker. Over seven decades, Barker and his successor, Robert Burford, presented 126 giant paintings in a circular hall in which patrons had a 360-degree perspective of scenery and depictions of recent battles as well as biblical scenes.[60]

At Niblo's Garden, Roberts's 2,000-foot-long canvas was one of several that fueled the new craze for such exhibitions, bringing customers to Niblo's outside of the warm summer months. Admission was 25 cents. The display changed on a tri-monthly basis. It was followed by John Martin's "Belshazzar's Feast," also 2,000 feet long. Panoramas were popular in many other parts of the city. The Coliseum, on Chambers Street near City Park, was a circular structure in which the patrons were spared exertion; when viewing the images on the walls, visitors were accommodated on a platform that revolved inside a structure that was later converted to the uses of the Croton Water Commission. Another formidable competitor to Niblo's exhibits was in a nearby brick structure on lots at Mercer and Prince Streets owned by John Jacob Astor. The immense building was designed and built specifically to accommodate a huge panorama of Jerusalem, created by Frederick Catherwood from his watercolor sketches during a journey to Palestine with fellow traveler John Lloyd Stephens.[61]

Pleasure gardens in New York mimicked their London contemporaries, but added distinctive American twists. Waxworks and *tableaux vivants* were spread among elegantly decorated boxes and bowers, separated by lantern-illuminated pathways. In New York, lurid depictions of female anatomy and scenes from the French Revolution were eschewed in these genteel environments, and even the nascent "Ethiopian" entertainments were more modest than in their heyday later in the century.[62]

Perhaps the most famous presentation of all during his first decade of pleasure garden operation resulted from Niblo's partnership with promoter P. T. Barnum. The two paired up in 1835 for the public display of "Joice Heth," an African American woman, supposedly 161 years old. Heth had been exhibited in Philadelphia most recently, alleged to have been George Washington's nurse. The New York venture was Barnum's first show in New York. He had applied earlier for a job as a bartender at Niblo's Saloon, but reconsidered when he discovered that Niblo was seeking a three-year commitment for the position. Barnum had come to New York City with the express intention of investing in some sort of public exhibition to make his living.[63] The nascent showman traveled to Philadelphia to view Heth, and found her to be blind, immobile, seemingly "a thousand years old," but extremely voluble and eager to sing the Baptist hymns of her own childhood as well as recount her years with young Washington, in the employ of his father, Augustine. Heth even claimed to have been present at the first president's birth.

On August 6, 1835, Barnum paid $1,000 to Kentuckian R. W. Lindsay to take control of the latter's relationship with Heth, and then continued her exhibition in Philadelphia for one more week. Barnum then reapproached Niblo (who, Barnum claimed, did not recognize him as a previous applicant for the bartending position), and the two made a deal to display Heth in a room in Niblo's home, adjacent to the saloon. Barnum had found the adjacent outdoor spaces positively charming, with their globe-illuminated pathways, elaborate plantings, and a series of seven-foot-tall, two-foot-wide transparencies decorating the sides of many paths. With the added draw of Niblo's Garden's outdoor amenities, Barnum fixed upon the indoor space for the Heth exhibition. Niblo agreed to provide lighting and a ticket seller, and pay for printing bills and other advertising, in exchange for fifty percent of the proceeds.

Crowds flocked to the exhibit, both in New York and other cities, and Barnum's career as showman and promoter took off like a rocket. Attendance grew even more after Barnum employed his assistant, Levi Lyman, to introduce Heth, answer spectators' questions, and write an illustrated souvenir pamphlet of Heth's history, which Barnum sold for six cents. Proceeds soon reached $1,500 per week as the New York newspapers took note of the show and audiences swelled. The ancient lady lay on a bed, smoked her pipe (as she claimed had been her habit for twelve decades), and beat time to church music, accompanied by a Baptist minister. Barnum took Heth to Providence, Boston, New Haven, and Albany before returning with her to New York and installing her in a hall at Bowery and Division Streets. She died in February 1836.

Unfortunately, Niblo's career was not the only thing propelled upward during his success with Barnum. The second floor of the building in which Joice Heth was displayed was devoted to the manufacture of the pyrotechnic materials frequently employed at the Garden. Tragedy struck mid-day on September 17, 1835: "Crimson fire" in a bottle capped with leather accidentally exploded in the Diorama building. The entire structure—Niblo's Saloon and the old amphitheater—together with the stored Roberts panorama was destroyed. Niblo's adjoining home at 576 Broadway also burned, though not to the ground. An African American man, Isaac Freeman, suffocated and was burned to death while assisting two firemen, who escaped.[64] Damage was not total. The furniture in Niblo's home was saved, as well as the garden and its plants and shrubbery. Niblo's loss was estimated at $7,500, excluding the $3,000 value of Roberts's masterpiece.[65] The 1835 fire did not end panoramic exhibitions at Niblo's Garden, however. In the 1840s, even larger scenes were displayed at an adjacent structure named the Panorama Building.[66]

Though wags and wiseacres predicted the end of Niblo's establishment, his popularity and entrepreneurial enthusiasm were vastly underestimated, and within a short time the debris of the old saloon and amphitheater was cleared and new and more solid structures erected. The saloon was reduced in size to permit the erection of a proscenium theater entirely separate from the ball and concert rooms. Frescoes by Signor Capelli adorned the new theater, but a trelliswork separated the extensive outdoor portions of the saloon from paying theatergoers. Niblo's bar was once again the place to see and be seen, especially in the summer months. The scents of mint juleps, sherry cobblers, and other "sweet-smelling decoctions" filled the warm nighttime air, and only rarely did the sounds of discord among competing beaux obtrude. According to Col. Thomas Picton, "the visitors at Niblo's bar were as much distinguished for the suavity of their manners as from the frequency of their potations."[67]

Visitors to Niblo's Garden entered a veritable paradise, safely removed from the stench and clatter of Broadway. Selina Watson, daughter of historian and author John Fanning Watson (1779–1860), took her first trip to New York from Germantown, Pennsylvania, as a young woman in October 1837. Her diary recounts her favorable impression of Niblo's, though she rated it only second best of its kind in New York:

> ... whent to see Niblo's garden; It was most beautiful but in my opinion It did not surpass Castle Garden. It was surprising that man could invent any thing so magnificent. The walks were laid out in the most complete order, but the Autumnal leave's had entirely coverd them. The path's on both side's had transparent pyrimads which in the evening was lightd up which presented to the eye of the beholder a most beautiful appearance. In the centre of this vast garden was a room which was hung all around with pictures of different discription's. the floor of this room was painted in wreaths of flowers; in the middle was a chandelier which was hung around with small lamp's of differant colours. and to add to the beauty, was a green house.[68]

During the months preceding the 1839 warm-weather season, a substantial improvement was added to the grounds of the Garden. This supplemented the rebuilding necessitated by the 1835 fire, and was announced by an advertisement in *The Evening Star* in New York City on June 7, 1839:

> Wm. Niblo respectfully announces to the public that this Establishment is now open for the Season. During the recess, a new and ELEGANT SALOON has been built, capable of holding two thousand persons, opening into the Garden by spacious galleries, where the charms of Music will receive new delight with the fragrant breeze from varied flowers and plants. The seats are backed and cushioned with rich damask. The establishments and decorations are executed by a celebrated artist.
>
> The greatest attention has been paid to ventilating the building, which, *en un mot,* is pronounced the most unique and elegant establishment in the country.
>
> The Gardens have been completely renovated, and all that the brilliancy of Lamps, the fragrance of flowers, and the charms of music can impart, may be enjoyed in this delightful spot.

Performances at the Garden were a varied lot: music of all kinds was mixed with acrobatics and vaudeville scenes. In the earliest years of the Garden, audience preferences for popular music from British traditions prevailed, with Italian operatic offerings sprinkled in. Madame Otto warbled such ballads as "By the Margin of Fair Zurich's Waters" and "Meet Me by Moonlight Alone" in summer evening programs, interspersed with daring acts by aerialist Il Antonio Diavolo and his troupe of children and the famed Alessandro Gambati doing solos on the brass instruments. Opera was already being performed sporadically in New York by the late 1820s, but Madame Otto and her offerings filled the role of the great European operatic sopranos like Maria Malibran until American tastes and skills matured.[69] The Ravel family of acrobats performed at the Garden frequently in the late 1830s and through the 1840s, interspersed with short theatrical runs that were benefits for the financial support of major thespians of the day. Gradual improvements were made to the Garden's physical plant: In 1837, the entrance to the saloon from the north end of the site on Broadway was covered and the auditorium enclosed so that inclement weather would not cause postponements. Means to heat the enclosed space were not provided, though, and the season at Niblo's continued to end with the onset of cool weather each year.

Niblo's Garden also proved popular as a military training ground when the need arose, and the neighborhood was the site of many public celebrations of military and ethnic/religious occasions. Col. Storms's horse artillery regiment practiced on what were christened the "Military Grounds," until it relocated to the site of the former Jefferson Market Courthouse. The Pulaski Cadets, founded in 1833 by disgruntled members of Col. William Tompkins's "Blues" (aka "The New York Light Guard"), made their home at Niblo's on the Crosby Street frontage, from which they marched forth in elaborate plumed uniforms to many parades.[70]

The Prince Street entrance to Niblo's Garden stood opposite Montgomery Hall, a bastion of Hibernian pride. For many years on St. Patrick's Day, bands of Irish men and women congregated there, and led a procession about town festooned with the traditional Irish colors and symbols. The marchers reached City Hall and then returned to the vicinity of the old St. Patrick's Cathedral on the corner of Mott and Prince Streets. Niblo had a long-standing relationship with the Irish American community and its annual celebrations in New York City. Katy Matheson's account is illuminating:

Dinner gatherings are an appropriate starting point since Niblo himself began his career as a caterer. Throughout the history of Niblo's Garden, dinner gatherings of various kinds—frequently political—took place there. One was the annual St. Patrick's Day gathering held by the Society of the Friendly Sons of St. Patrick. Both Niblo and his brother were members of this organization, which was not at that time strongly identified with Catholicism since it preceded the large immigration of Irish Catholics at the time of the famine. This annual gathering had been held at Niblo's Bank Coffee House from 1818 to 1831. In 1832 it was moved to Niblo's Saloon . . . It was held again at Niblo's in 1840, this time listed as Niblo's "Tavern." It would be held at the facilities of the Metropolitan Hotel in later years (1857–62, 1878, and in 1882 at "Niblo's Saloon" there). According to newspaper accounts, the Saturday, March 17, 1832 gathering was attended by "about sixty members and several guests." The accounts also note the "sumptuous dinner prepared by Mr. Niblo," and further that "the table was bountifully laded and decorated with appropriate devices." The only other hints given about the environment of the dinner are a comment about the "spacious saloon" and a description of an occurrence early in the evening's activities:

. . . a curtain fell from the wall of the Saloon, and to the eyes of all, was exhibited a very brilliant and tasteful transparency; it represented a flagpole in a horizontal position, from which gracefully undulated the American Banner, and on which was perched the Bald Eagle, our country's emblem, and underneath was printed the following motto: PROTECTION TO THE SONS OF THE EMERALD ISLE. It was a happy device and was received with applause.

The rest of the evening's activities included toasting, drinking, and singing, with a series of some thirteen "regular" toasts, each followed by an appropriate patriotic song, as well as some twenty-one "volunteer" toasts.

The similarity of this gathering to one four years earlier at the Bank Coffee House is noteworthy. Held in the long-room of that tavern, the banquet featured a sumptuous dinner as well as thirteen "regular" toasts and some twenty-three "volunteer" toasts, interspersed with patriotic songs. According to vividly detailed accounts, the decor combined both Irish and American symbols such as a transparency of St. Patrick and an eagle bearing an Irish harp, the shield of the United States, an olive branch, arrows, and a garland of shamrocks.[71]

In the early years of Niblo's Garden, much of the Broadway frontage nearby remained vacant, and the masses of visitors to Niblo's establishments created opportunities for other watering holes and circuses that could attract the custom of men and women drawn way uptown for the day and/or evening. Directly across Broadway, on the western side of the muck-ridden thoroughfare, lay a series of lots whose muddy ponds and briars formed an inviting repose, according to one memoirist, "in which the strolling porkers of the neighborhood laid recumbent until the decline of the sunshine warned them of the hour of their homeward journey." Abundant feral pigs still wandered the streets of lower Manhattan in the early 1830s, and apparently ventured far from the center of town during the day. In the midst of the same lots, hidden behind a row of well-trimmed poplars, stood the brightly painted enclosures of a neat and brilliant ale house, whose patrons perhaps could not afford the tariffs of Niblo's genteel saloon. The ale house in question was run by a Frenchman who specialized in Albany cream ale, which was dispensed in growlers to African American servants every Sunday in copious quantities, to be lugged home to the sabbath tables of the gentry who had sat through long, dry morning church sermons without respite or refreshment. Ditto, in all likelihood, the taps of the Bell Tavern and Toby Philpot's, which sat on the east side of Broadway in the same blocks.[72]

In its first incarnation, the arena-cum-amphitheater of Niblo's Garden played various roles in the entertainment life of the young city, among which was to host the throngs of upwardly mobile younger men and women who disdained the stratified and exclusive dancing assemblies held in prior decades in the City Hotel by the Park. Social regimentation and physical restraint had long characterized these chaperoned, regimented, downtown get-togethers. The first stirrings of the women's rights movement and the evanescence of the so-called sporting gentlemen's societies fueled the passion to dance in a less supervised environment. At first, Washington Hall hosted the more liberal gatherings, denominated "publics," at 280 Broadway. That hall was located on the northeast corner of Broadway and Chambers Street, where A. T. Stewart's first large department store was later built in 1842. Rival dancing masters encouraged their students to try to outshine those of their competitors at these gatherings, and charitable organizations soon seized upon sponsorship of such events as fund-raising opportunities with mixed company present, a powerful driver for many charities. Niblo's Garden, with its vast

FIGURE 20: *Annual Fair of the American Institute at Niblo's Garden c. 1845 by Benjamin Johns Harrison; collection of the Museum of the City of New York.*

arena, opened at the onset of these new customs. Though the premises were poorly enclosed for the cold-weather season, Niblo's nonetheless became instantly popular for the "ball of the Kusckiusko [sic] Cadets, the crack cohort of the town, who, by the way, maintained an armory upon Niblo's domain." According to Col. Thomas Picton, "Niblo's was voted the only place wherein charitable dancing, civil and military, could be accomplished strictly *comme il faut*."[73]

Niblo added another innovation to the "publics" held at his Garden. In the high-society balls of the early nineteenth century as well as in the earliest "publics" elsewhere, refreshments were brought in by the servants of the more distinguished guests. For those lacking servants, the obligation to retrieve cakes and punch from serving tables—and then balance their ladies' choices upon the suitors' laps upon cambric handkerchiefs—made the introduction of Niblo's Saloon and its formal offerings and generously available furniture most welcome. A separate supper room was set up for balls, and at the stroke of midnight, the band would sound a characteristic promenade, whereupon each beau would lead his lady into the elegantly festooned gallery space, where tables groaned with sumptuous platters and all necessary appliances to enjoy them. A colonnaded and lantern-illuminated bridge stretched over a portion of the crowded Garden grounds to the Prince Street entrance and became the preferred stroll in the years before the first of several fires at the site.[74]

Outside the busiest summer months, Niblo provided accommodations for many kinds of public presentations. As early as October 1834, the American Institute Fair began renting the grounds to display the latest developments in technology and industry.[75] The Fair began as a short exposition of a few days, but quickly grew to two weeks, "a decided event, systematically anticipated and habitually chronicled by the press as an occurrence of a national celebration."[76] The Fair took over much of Niblo's site—so much so that in 1841 when portions of a two-story building on Crosby Street were rented out for three years by Niblo to Allen Leonard and John Steele for use as a billiard parlor, Niblo reserved the right to preempt that use for 18 days each year for the American Institute Fair. In other years his income from the lease to the American Institute was well known enough to be the object of an attempted attachment in a suit by a creditor over nonpayment of Niblo's debts.[77]

Many "firsts" were recorded at Niblo's Garden. On July 18, 1837, Nib-

FIGURE 21: *William Burton's Theater; Collection of The New-York Historical Society.*

lo announced the American premiere of "Les Vaudevilles," a Parisian form of short theatrical entertainments often presented with French titles.[78] According to theater historian George C. D. Odell, the 1837 season at Niblo's marked the first true theatrical season there, when vaudevilles were presented on certain nights interspersed with acrobatic shows by the Ravels and other forms of stage entertainment.[79]

Niblo's reputation as the premier and most magnificent venue for any large public celebration made easy the task of the New York branch of the St. George Society when it came time to mount a local celebration of Queen Victoria's wedding to Prince Albert in 1840. The New York chapter of the Society became vexed when the young queen consented to allow her portrait to be painted by a Philadelphian, Thomas Sully, and the New Yorkers resolved to one-up their Philadelphia brethren with Niblo's help. A military concert, free dinner (including an ox, roasted whole) for widows and orphans of the society, a grand gentlemen's dinner, and an even larger ball were mounted, complete with skyrockets. All went off in a blaze of glory, excepting the ox, which proved as stubborn in death as it was docile in life: the beast's flesh refused to roast, either whole or in quarters, and the free dinner failed. A copy of an article about the event in the weekly *Albion* was printed in gold upon satin and forwarded to the

FIGURE 22: *Laura Keene's Theater; Collection of The New-York Historical Society.*

young marrieds with New Yorkers' best wishes.[80]

Day-to-day management of the facility was often vested by Niblo in third parties, and the Garden was rented out to individual artists and other impresarios alike.[81] When New York's National Theater burned down in late September 1839, the prominent actor James Wallack, Sr. (who had been the lessee and manager of the National) removed his entire company to Niblo's Garden. Within one week, Wallack secured the famed thespian Charles Kean to play Richard III, ensuring large crowds and financial success.

Other managers and lessees of Niblo's controlled the actual productions presented on his stage during the 1830s through 1846: John Sefton, Wardle Corbyn, William Wheatley, and others presented shows ranging from Shakespeare to now long-forgotten light American fare. The greatest thespians of the day mounted Niblo's stage. During these years, Charlotte Cushman, Joseph Jefferson, John Sefton, William Burton, James Wallack, Sr., Edmund Kean, Charles Kemble, Edwin Forrest, Charles Kean, Edwin Booth, and Henry Irving all performed at Niblo's. Many nights were devoted to "benefits" for a particular actor or actress, it being understood that the wages of these popular figures and their sometimes dissolute lifestyles frequently left many in dire straits. Even

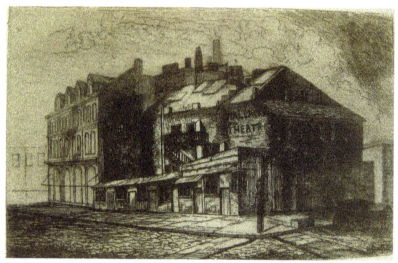

FIGURE 23: *James Wallack's Theater; Collection of The New-York Historical Society.*

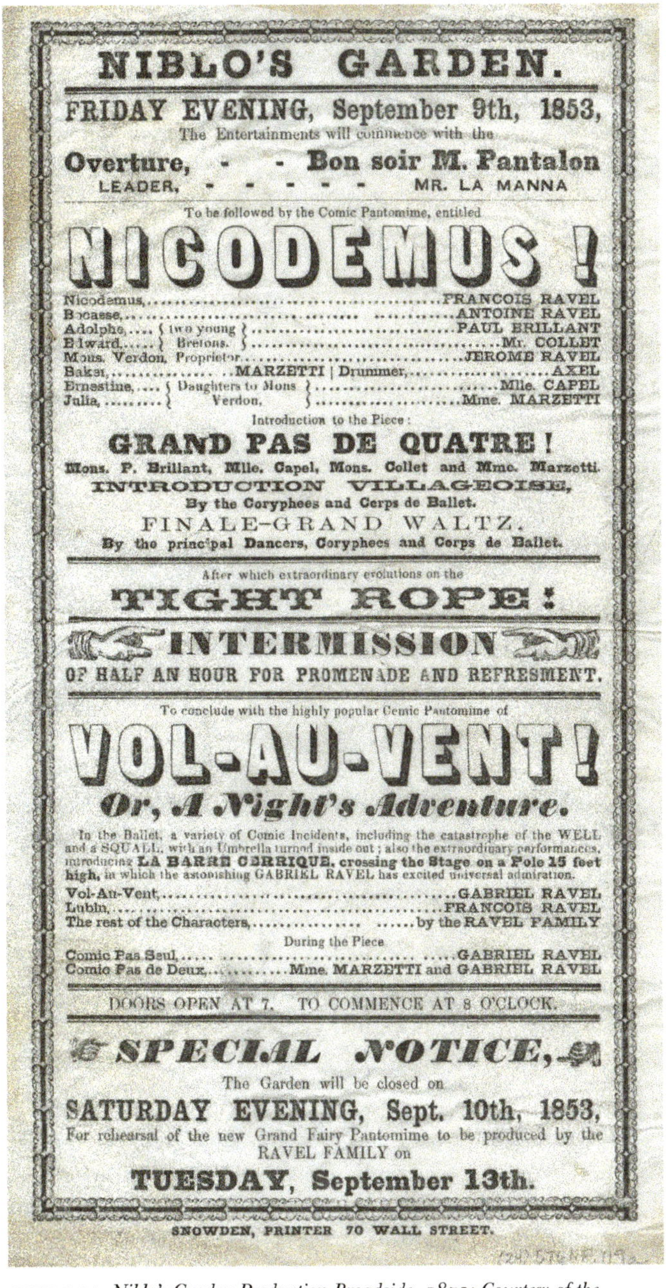

NIBLO'S GARDEN.

FRIDAY EVENING, September 9th, 1853,

The Entertainments will commence with the

Overture, - - Bon soir M. Pantalon

LEADER, - - - - - - MR. LA MANNA

To be followed by the Comic Pantomime, entitled

NICODEMUS!

Nicodemus,..FRANCOIS RAVEL
Bocasse,..ANTOINE RAVEL
Adolphe,.... { two young } ....PAUL BRILLANT
Edward,..... { Bretons. } ....Mr. COLLET
Mons. Verdon, Proprietor..............................JEROME RAVEL
Baker,................MARZETTI | Drummer,........................AXEL
Ernestine,.... { Daughters to Mons } ....Mlle. CAPEL
Julia,........ { Verdon, } ....Mme. MARZETTI

Introduction to the Piece:

GRAND PAS DE QUATRE!

Mons. P. Brillant, Mlle. Capel, Mons. Collet and Mme. Marzetti.

INTRODUCTION VILLAGEOISE,

By the Coryphees and Corps de Ballet.

FINALE–GRAND WALTZ.

By the principal Dancers, Coryphees and Corps de Ballet.

After which extraordinary evolutions on the

TIGHT ROPE!

INTERMISSION

OF HALF AN HOUR FOR PROMENADE AND REFRESHMENT.

To conclude with the highly popular Comic Pantomime of

VOL-AU-VENT!

Or, A Night's Adventure.

In the Ballet, a variety of Comic Incidents, including the catastrophe of the WELL and a SQUALL, with an Umbrella turned inside out; also the extraordinary performances, introducing LA BARRE CERRIQUE, crossing the Stage on a Pole 15 feet high, in which the astonishing GABRIEL RAVEL has excited universal admiration.

Vol-Au-Vent,..GABRIEL RAVEL
Lubin,..FRANCOIS RAVEL
The rest of the Characters,........................by the RAVEL FAMILY

During the Piece

Comic Pas Seul,..GABRIEL RAVEL
Comic Pas de Deux,............Mme. MARZETTI and GABRIEL RAVEL

DOORS OPEN AT 7. TO COMMENCE AT 8 O'CLOCK.

SPECIAL NOTICE,

The Garden will be closed on

SATURDAY EVENING, Sept. 10th, 1853,

For rehearsal of the new Grand Fairy Pantomime to be produced by the RAVEL FAMILY on

TUESDAY, September 13th.

SNOWDEN, PRINTER 70 WALL STREET.

FIGURE 24: *Niblo's Garden Production Broadside, 1853; Courtesy of the Library Company of Philadelphia.*

Mr. and Mrs. Niblo held benefits for themselves in the late 1830s and early 1840s.[82]

The popularity of Niblo's Garden was immense even in its first decade of operation. Three nights a week were devoted to Italian operatic offerings during the summer season of 1834. A terrible heat wave in mid-July brought crowds to the saloon, and "the havoc committed among the ice-creams and pitchers of lemonade [was] really awful," according to an editorial in the *New-York Mirror*.[83] Over a series of evenings in late August 1834, a famous trumpet competition between Englishman John Thompson Norton and Italian Alessandro Gambati brought thousands of their devotees to Niblo's, many decked out in the favored colors of their performers. The Campagnologian Bell Ringers arrived in 1837 to great acclaim. Besides the Ravel family of French acrobats, who performed dozens of times at Niblo's, so did Herr Cline and other aerialists and experts at legerdemain. The Ravels, who frequently took nonfamily members into their troupe (including the later world-famous Charles Blondin, and Leon Javelli), remained favorites at Niblo's for decades thereafter. Their shows were a mixture of ballet, pantomime, spoken theatrics, and acrobatics.[84]

What would today be considered high-brow culture knew no class boundaries in New York in the early decades of the nineteenth century. As in Shakespeare's day, his plays were well attended by men of all stations in life, literate and illiterate alike. Many of the Bard's works were committed to memory by Bowery B'hoys and other ruffians who delighted in attending the shows in venues far less genteel than Niblo's and shouting out the completion of lines in advance of famed players' recitations. Likewise, Italian opera took America by storm in the 1830s: *New-York Mirror* wrote on August 23, 1834: "Now the very sweep-boys whistle Rossini, as they tramp along the streets, and correctly, too."

The fortunes of Italian opera waxed and waned in New York City, but 1843 marked an upsurge in popularity with the September 15 American premiere of Donizetti's *Lucia di Lammermoor* at Niblo's. *Norma* was also presented that season at Niblo's.

Even though there was no heating system in the auditorium, Niblo decided to expand his season at the end of 1840, introducing a series of "concerts d'hiver" for the winter of 1840–1. A rudimentary enclosure to the hall proved reasonably adequate that winter and in succeeding seasons. Summers continued to be best for business, though. The American debut of the polka was danced at Niblo's in a sketch entitled "Polkamania," on June 17, 1844.[85] Low-brow circus took over Niblo's during the fall and winter of 1843–4: An equestrian troupe accompanied by acrobats, high-wire artists, tumblers, and the like performed there in various combinations beginning at the end of November. A group of supposed Bedouin Arabs and traditional clowns rounded out the presentations, admission to which cost fifty cents.[86]

The mid-1840s proved inauspicious for Niblo, despite his raging success. Unfortunately, the fire of September 17, 1835, was only a precursor to a more serious conflagration: Eleven years later, to the day, calamity struck again, though the indomitable Niblo would carry on.

Chapter 4
DISASTER AND REBIRTH

~~~>●<~~~

With the waning daylight hours of the end of the summer of 1846, Niblo's Garden announced that its doors would open thirty minutes earlier than usual, starting September 18. A rich program was advertised for that evening, which would benefit Gabriel Ravel, head of the popular French troupe. *Le Gascon a Trois Visages* (translated by the advertiser as "Stratagem Better than Force") headed the bill, followed by the Ravel company's ever-popular "Bedouin Arabs." The program would end with a comic pantomime by Robert Betrand.[87]

At 4:00 a.m. the cry of "fire" was heard. In the "Green-Room" where tickets were sold through a street-side aperture in a wall, the flames quickly spread to the stage, scenery, and boxes, enveloping the structure in a "bright sheet of flame," according to the next morning's *Tribune*.[88]

Fans of the Ravels would have to rely on their imaginations in lieu of the scheduled performance: "The scene looked like a Titanic exhibition of Pyrotechny, and one almost waited to hear the shouts of applause that were to greet some Polyphemus Ravel as he appeared on a hawse-cable stretched from Orion to the Pleiades."[89] The conflagration swept away the concert hall and reduced the gardens to a "barren waste of wilted trees and smoke-dyed rubbish," in the memory of one contemporary.[90]

Niblo suffered serious financial consequences when the entire complex was destroyed.[91] His personal offices at the Garden, decorated with his extensive art collection, were consumed in the flames, though a good bit of his household furniture and his most important financial records were salvaged by one of his neighbors, who rushed in with the late-arriving fire companies. Even with the staggering losses, there was no doubt about rebuilding. Niblo's lease with the Van Rensselaer estate would have to be renegotiated, though, as its term had only 18 months left to run. The Ravel family lost all of their costumes, props, music, and the rest of the season's proceeds, valued at $15,000 to $20,000.[92]

FIGURE 25: *Edwin Forrest.*   FIGURE 26: *William Macready.*

The only building that did not burn to the ground had a bowling alley on the first floor, and on the second the armory of the City Guard, a militia whose muskets were removed before the flames reached them. Among the other casualties of the blaze was the American Institute Fair, which had to relocate indefinitely. Four days after the fire, the *Tribune* surmised that arson was involved, as was also suspected in recent attempts to burn the Greenwich Theater on Charlton Street as well as the Mott Iron Works (location unidentified in the article) and stables in Burton Street.[93]

The fire may have destroyed Niblo's main enterprise, but his name and reputation remained intact. Within fourteen months, he had secured a new hall, one block south on Broadway, and was presenting blackface minstrelsy at Alhamra [sic] Hall, which he also advertised as "Niblo's Saloon" at number 559. "The Original Western and Southern Band of Sable Harmonists," under the direction of Thomas Sproull, had a substantial run during the week of November 24, 1847, competing with similar offerings at the better-known Christy's Minstrels down Broadway, as well as with the multitude of other racist spoofs along downtown's antebellum theater row.[94] During the summer of 1848, Niblo and thespian James H. Hackett leased the year-old Astor Place Opera House for a warm-weather season of Viennese dancers, singers, and farce. The eve-

FIGURE 27: *Astor Place Opera House, c. 1849; Courtesy of New York Public Library Digital Images Collection.*

ning of July 22 offered a program of musical drama, pantomime, and ballet with the Lehman family. Its young star, Mlle Adelaide (aka Adeline and Adele), offered a *grand pas des deux* from *Giselle* with M. Schmidt.[95] Adelaide became a popular member of the Niblo coterie of performers until Christmastime 1850, when tragedy would befall her.

Niblo's involvement with the Astor Place Opera House lasted well into 1849, as he marked time until the planned opening of the totally new Niblo's Garden on July 30. The infamously bloody Astor Place riot that took place on May 10 inside and outside the hall during his tenure as lessee demonstrated the resilience of his reputation and marked a watershed in American cultural affairs.[96]

Since colonial times, Americans of every class and background had been fierce devotees of Shakespeare's work. Literate or not, New Yorkers attended theaters downtown where many of his works were in repertory, and the same company performed several different plays each week. Nativist politics informed the cultural landscape of New York in the early decades of Niblo's career as a theater impresario, and gangs of Bowery B'hoys flocked to the stalls to cheer their favorite American-born actors holding forth as Macbeth or Richard III, while hissing and booing com-

FIGURE 28: *The Astor Place Opera House Riot, May 10, 1849; Courtesy of New York Public Library.*

petitors from the English stage, with rotten tomatoes aimed and fired far above their well-shod feet.

Edwin Forrest was one such Yankee favorite. Born in Philadelphia in 1806, Forrest had his professional debut at age 14 after a series of inconsequential apprenticeships in trade. By the age of 21, he had performed at the popular Bowery Theater in New York as Othello and shuttled back and forth between New York and Philadelphia, filling major roles. Forrest's trip to London in 1836 lasted ten months, and his Shakespearean performances at the Drury Lane and elsewhere, as well as his mentorship by Britain's beloved William Macready and Charles Kemble, boded well for an international career.

The seeds of the Astor Place riot were sown in 1845, however, when Londoners hissed Forrest as Macbeth during his second tour there. Though Forrest had been helped by Macready during the American's first English visit, Forrest attributed the disrespect to Macready and his fans, who deemed the Yankee's physical appearance and acting style unsuitable. A few weeks later, as Macready played Hamlet in Edinburgh, Forrest stood up in a private box and returned the insults, hissing the popular Englishman; he followed up with a derogatory letter to the Lon-

55

don *Times*. Better-educated American Shakespeare devotees also looked down upon some of the cruder theatrics that Forrest employed upon occasion, preferring the classic style of Macready when he came to New York. Macready was a frequent visitor to America, and a substantial rivalry grew between the two camps.

John Sefton and William Chippendale, who were associated with Niblo and Hackett's 1848 summer shows, were reemployed by them for an early May presentation by Macready at the Astor Place venue. Hackett, known as the American Falstaff, was also a long-standing enemy of Edwin Forrest, and tensions ran high.[97] The appetite of New Yorkers for Shakespeare was well evidenced by the fact that on the evening of May 7, three productions of *Macbeth* were scheduled in Manhattan: Macready at the Astor Place, Forrest at the Broadway Theatre, and Thomas Hamblin at the Bowery Theater. A tide of politically infused protest rose in the press and via public petitions and broadsides, with upper-crust and Whig supporters of Macready denouncing the vulgarity of Forrest. Nativists countered with charges that Macready's supporters desired that Great Britain once again rule over America. Anti-Macready feeling caused a unification of New York ruffians thought impossible: nativist Bowery B'hoys united with their hated Irish gang rivals to rally against Macready, all in the name of Americanism.[98]

Niblo and Hackett took the precaution of boarding up the windows of the Opera House before the scheduled performance. Fearing that the rumored disturbances would lead to violence and property damage, Mayor Woodhull ordered the removal of piles of paving stones in the area where sewer construction was under way, and summoned the theater operators and various law enforcement officials to his offices on the morning of May 10. The mayor, though admitting his lack of authority to prevent Niblo and Hackett from going forward with that evening's show, nonetheless asked the partners to cancel the performance. Niblo and Hackett instead asked for protection, and the mayor called upon General Sandford of the New York State Militia to keep troops in readiness to supplement the New York City municipal police if trouble broke out. It did.

By 6:00 p.m., 325 policemen had arrived at the site, the majority of whom were stationed at various points inside the Opera House. The balance ringed the perimeter of the structure and two adjacent buildings. Two hundred militiamen were mustered to positions further downtown.[99] Over one hundred admissions had been purchased by nativist troublemakers, but when the doors to the theater opened, most were barred, as their tickets lacked a special mark arranged by Macready supporters to exclude those unfriendly to the star. A few miscreants snuck in, though, and immediately started a ruckus. Arrested by police inside the theater, they were locked up in a storage room under the parquet, but the ruffians promptly set a small fire, and as smoke seeped into the auditorium, a major disturbance erupted. Somehow the flames were stamped out, order restored, and the second act of *Macbeth* began. Outside, a riot ensued, with paving stones (gathered despite the mayor's earlier directives) hurled at will. Planks were torn from the Opera House windows, and shattered glass filled the streets and lobby of the theater. Macready soldiered on, mocking the mob with the Bard's own words from Act V, Scene 5: "Our castle's strength will laugh a siege to scorn." General Sandford's troops were called into place, but their stolid front only inflamed the rioters more, and total mayhem ensued. With the guards' backs to the theater, the order to fire was given, and bullets flew everywhere. Notoriously inaccurate, the fusillade from the long arms downed random passersby as well as rioters. At least eight dozen soldiers and civilians were injured, and 20 deaths occurred. Fifty-three rioters were arrested and held in jail the day after. Virtually every window in each façade of the opera house was shattered, and bullet holes sprinkled its exterior walls as well as those of many nearby buildings.[100] Local pharmacies and saloons were used as temporary morgues. Macready managed to don a disguise as a militiaman, and slip out of the theater unnoticed in the crowd as throngs howled for his neck. A horse was at the ready, and he galloped to New Rochelle and caught the first train to Boston on the morning of May 11.[101]

Outrage at the riot was aimed in many directions. Rumors abounded the next morning of a second disturbance, incited by the many deaths and injuries and hatred for the militia and police who were deemed culpable in what many saw as unnecessary gunfire and politically motivated reactions to the rowdy crowd. According to James Godron Ben-

FIGURE 29: *Interior of Opera House at Niblo's Garden c. 1860; Courtesy of New York Public Library Digital Images Collection.*

FIGURE 30: *The Ballroom at Niblo's Garden c. 1860; Collection of The New-York Historical Society.*

nett's *Herald*, which sold an unprecedented 33,500 copies on May 11, the conflagration was viewed by many as class warfare, a "collision between those who have been styled the 'exclusives,' or 'upper ten' and the great popular masses."

Placards were posted by the nativist supporters all over the city:

AMERICANS!
AROUSE! THE GREAT CRISIS
HAS COME!
Decide now whether English
ARISTOCRATS!!!
AND
FOREIGN RULE!!!
shall triumph on this
AMERICA'S METROPOLIS
or whether her own
SONS
whose fathers once compelled the base-born miscreants to succumb, shall meanly lick the hand that strikes, and allow themselves to be deprived of the liberty of opinion
so dear to every American heart.
AMERICANS!
come out and dare to own yourselves sons of the iron hearts
of '76!!

An estimated 20,000 to 25,000 persons assembled in City Hall Park that evening at 6:00 p.m., where the speechifying, led by prominent attorneys, went on and on. Other demonstrations assembled in two other city parks, but violence was avoided and things remained quiet thereafter.

Despite the carnage, the consequences for Niblo seem to have only been financial. His insistence on the enterprise being protected by the authorities, instead of kowtowing to threatened mob violence and canceling the show, was beyond serious reproach. Whether or not Niblo was a cultural supporter of Macready is unclear. Niblo was an Irishman, and a strong opponent of all things Whig. He had even forced the postponement of a concert at his Saloon some nine years previous when the featured artist attempted to include in his program "The Grand National Whig Song."[102] Politics were probably not the reason for his conduct in this case. Business was business, and Niblo's reputation did not seem to suffer as a result of the murderous fiasco.

The riot's aftermath dominated New York's consciousness for many months, but Niblo was not delayed in his larger enterprise by the aborted summer season on Astor Place. The grand opening of his expanded and far more elegant main theater and ancillary facilities at Niblo's Garden at the end of July required his utmost attention. Niblo's Garden, in its new incarnation, was grander and fancier than ever. The main theater dominated the site, with seating for two thousand and many private boxes, decorated in a style rivaling the grand opera houses of Europe. The Saloon was rebuilt with separate upper ladies' rooms and a lower gentleman's section, with appropriate differences in the beverages served. Supper rooms, a separate ballroom, and magnificent galleries and entrance halls and lobbies were filled with gilded ornamentation. The main theater's ceiling was domed, and caryatids and cupids were interspersed with golden wreaths and medallions on every available surface. The orchestra space was arranged to be easily adjustable in size to fit the scope

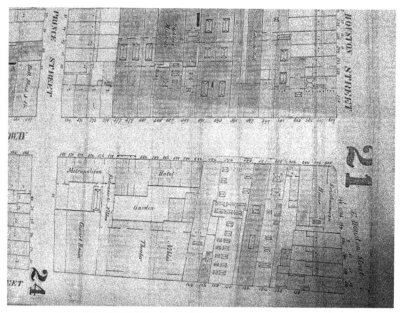

FIGURE 31: *Map of site of Niblo's Garden c. 1860 by William Perris; Courtesy of New York Public Library Digital Collections.*

of the stage production, whether ten or a hundred musicians were employed. Hot-air furnaces turned the new Niblo's Garden into a true year-round performance and event venue, remedying one of the chief shortcomings criticized in earlier years.[103] The poor ventilation of other Manhattan theaters during the hot summer months continued to give Niblo's Garden a decided advantage in warm weather. Its relatively open surroundings, even when the garden itself was mostly built over by parts of the Metropolitan Hotel in 1852, provided breezes into Niblo's buildings on the site that made for pleasant evenings indoors and out.

FIGURE 32: *Advertisement for Metropolitan Hotel (1852) from J. Milton Emerson,* Views in America, Great Britain, Switzerland, Turkey, Italy, the Holy Land Etc. *(J. Milton Emerson, New York: 1852).*

FIGURE 33: *Dinner at the Opening of the Metropolitan Hotel in Gleason's Pictorial (1852); Collection of The New-York Historical Society.*

FIGURE 34: *The Metropolitan Hotel c. 1860; Collection of The New-York Historical Society.*

The new facility opened on Tuesday, July 31, 1849, under the management of John Sefton and William Chippendale, the same individuals who managed Niblo's Garden before the fire. True to form, the ever-popular Ravel troupe opened the season with *The Milliners (or The Hungarian Rendezvous)* and *The Magic Trumpet (or The Invisible Harlequin)*. Niblo was taking no chances with his programming. Popularity and commercial viability governed his choices, as always.

FIGURE 35: *The Metropolitan Hotel c. 1878; Collection of The New-York Historical Society: Quinn Hotel Collection.*

The Ravels continued to expand their troupe and their presentations, becoming arguably the most popular show at Niblo's throughout the 1850s. Their pantomimes, as well as acrobatics and ballet, delighted New Yorkers year after year, together with their realization of vaudevilles.

Within 18 months after the glorious reopening of Niblo's Garden, tragedy struck again. During a Christmas Eve performance in 1850, 23-year-old Adelaide Lehman ascended a ladder at the side of the stage. Her dress caught fire from the lamps. Knowing that her cries would panic the audience and cause a stampede, the brave trouper kept silent as the curtain was rung down and a carpenter's baize jacket was wrapped around her in a desperate attempt to quench the flames. The crowd remained unaware, but Lehman died a few days later. In the New Year's Day words of the *Tribune*, "The flame, too enamored of the grace that rivaled its own litheness, had folded her in a fatal embrace."[104]

The site of Niblo's Garden underwent tremendous change with the construction of the gigantic Metropolitan Hotel, which began by mid-June of 1850. The L-shaped structure wrapped around Niblo's buildings, which maintained an ornate but narrow entrance on Broadway with a corridor through the block to the theater, concert room, and saloon whose façades continued to stand on Crosby and Prince Streets. The garden was accessible via the same corridor from Broadway but was much reduced in size from its spacious layout in prior decades. Niblo could not have been happy about the development, as the light and air to his premises were severely attenuated. There was no recourse, though: he had a mere leasehold interest in the parcel and did not control the rest of the block.

The blocks south of Astor Place were under rapid development in the early 1850s as New York's center of carriage-trade merchants, finest restaurants, and fanciest hotels of the antebellum period. Meanwhile, the tide of residential development catering to upper-middle-class and wealthier residents moved north to and beyond Union Square. The Metropolitan was designed by John Snook (architect of the first Grand Central railroad station, named then Grand Central Depot) and his partner, Joseph Trench, and built at a cost of $940,000 by P. S. Van Rensselaer, Esq. The hotel boasted steam heat, inter-floor speaking tubes, bells to summon attendants throughout the floors, and gas illumination in the elegant corridors. *The Scientific American* described the structure, leased to the Leland brothers, as the "most splendidly furnished hotel in the world; its interior resembles a fairy palace."[105] Its magnificent ballroom quickly became the preferred venue for large public events after the hotel opened on September 1, 1852.[106]

Programming at Niblo's entertainment complex was governed not so much by lofty artistic goals as by the desire to sell as many seats as possible at each event while catering to polite but popular taste. Niblo and his various managers relied upon well-known troupes, predominantly composed of European-born performers, to sell out the house, night after night in several-week runs, rather than booking one-night stands of famous actors and singers.[107] Bills from the 1850s show many dozens of performances by Max Maretzek's Italian Opera Company, the Pyne-Harrison Opera company, and the Ravels. The Ravel family brought the unknown Charles Blondin to the United States in 1853 as a member of their *corps de ballet*, seven years before his legendary crossing of Niagara Falls on a tightrope with an omelet pan and portable stove, used mid-crossing for a snack.[108]

Nonetheless, the most famous performers of the day did appear, especially when William Burton's company took over the Garden. Many thespians whose names would become household words appeared at Niblo's early in their careers, though infrequently thereafter. Charlotte Cushman, Edwin Booth (as a 26-year-old, playing Iago in *Othello*), and Matilda Heron all appeared there in the 1850s, and many members of the Wallack family played at the Garden before James Wallack, Sr., opened his own house.[109] The Spanish child prodigy soprano Adelina Patti, who became beloved across the United States, debuted in New York as a seven-year-old, holding her doll, singing the finale, "Ah, non giunge," from the third act of *La Sonnambula* on Niblo's stage on December 3, 1851.[110]

Competition for the theatergoer's pocket was intense: Up and down Broadway, from Canal Street to Astor Place, a theater district grew up, far from the few downtown venues that antedated the reopening of Niblo's Garden. By 1859, James Wallack's Theater and Laura Keene's, as well as Bryant's Minstrels, Fellows Opera House, Henry Wood's Marble Hall,

FIGURE 36: *West Side of Broadway near Prince Street, looking north, c. 1860; Courtesy of New York Public Library Digital Collections.*

Tripler Hall, and several others were operating within a few blocks of Niblo's Garden.[111] Grand opera was also presented near Union Square at the Academy of Music beginning in 1854 as well as at Palmo's Opera House, built in 1844 in Chambers Street by a former pastry chef named Ferdinand Palmo, and converted four years later, after Palmo's failure, by William Burton to his eponymous theater.[112]

Circus acts, especially equestrian extravaganzas, continued a tradition that predated Niblo's acquisition of the site. New York had hosted menageries and tented circuses since the late eighteenth century, with the larger operations frequently situating themselves on the outskirts of what was then the settled part of the city. Wealthy men's stables, equestrian training schools, and circuses occupied the site of Niblo's Garden and adjacent properties before his Sans Souci opened in 1828. Prancing horse-flesh continued on the site, even after the disastrous fire of 1846 and the construction of the splendid enclosed opera house. Byron's *Mazzeppa* filled Niblo's in December 1852, with the human performers' talents outshone, in one commentator's opinion, by the skills of General Welch's horses and ponies in the show.[113]

The year 1855 was particularly memorable for patrons of Niblo's

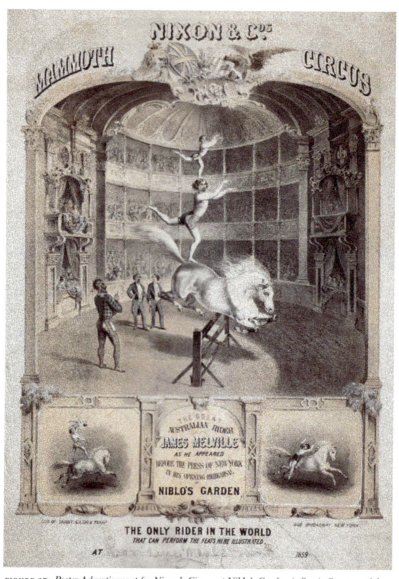

FIGURE 37: *Poster Advertisement for Nixon's Circus at Niblo's Garden (1859); Courtesy of the American Antiquarian Society.*

Garden. On February 25, the bandleader who had traditionally accompanied the Ravels' shows returned for a musical extravaganza. Harvey Dodworth and his Monster Band and Grand Chorus filled the house; Dodworth would become one of the greatest military band leaders and composers of Civil War marches.

FIGURE 38: *Courtyard of Niblo's Garden as part of Metropolitan Hotel c. 1861; Courtesy of New York Public Library Digital Collections*

September 1 that same year saw a benefit for Herr Andre (aka John) Cline, the Seiltänzer (tightrope walker), who had first performed his rope dancing feats at the Sans Souci 27 years prior. On September 27, the premiere of one of the first operas written by and about Americans began a run that extended through the rest of 1855. *Rip Van Winkle* was a wild success with New Yorkers. Composer/maestro George F. Bristow and librettist John Wainwright's production featured George Stretton, late of Drury Lane, Covent Garden, and the Royal Philharmonic of London, in the title role (reprised by New Yorkers' favorite, Joseph Jefferson, in later years) and Louisa Pyne as Alice. The opera played 18 times before the end of the year to enormous critical acclaim. A benefit performance was held on Saturday evening, October 6, for the victims of a yellow fever plague at Norfolk

FIGURE 39: *Courtyard of Niblo's Garden as part of Metropolitan Hotel c. 1861; Courtesy of New York Public Library Digital Collections*

67

FIGURE 40: *Japanese Delegation Entering Carriages In Front of Metropolitan Hotel June 18, 1860; Courtesy of the New York Public Library Digital Collections.*

FIGURE 41: *"Tommy" and friends with a New York City lady; Courtesy of The Collection of Tom Burnett.*

FIGURE 42: *The Ball at Niblo's Garden; from* Harper's Illustrated Weekly, *June, 1860.*

and Portsmouth, Virginia, chaired by Mayor Fernando Wood and a host of civic luminaries.[114]

Admission prices remained remarkably constant at Niblo's Garden during the 1850s: Fifty cents gained entrance to the orchestra seats, slightly more for the parquet level; and for $5, a private box could be secured, seating six, whereby parents could keep close watch on their children. Ten such boxes were added when the main theater was renovated from top to bottom and reopened in early May 1854.[115] Performances by especially popular female opera singers could command more. Single seats to hear Mesdames Marietta Alboni and Henrietta Sontag were considerably more dear.[116]

Profits stood foremost in Niblo's mind down to the last months of his active management of the theater. Previous disasters with a given performer were no bar to re-presentation, provided popular sentiment was

FIGURE 43: *Mrs. Watson Sheet Music; Courtesy of The New York Public Library Digital Images Collection*

assured. Perhaps the strangest example involved Edwin Forrest. On September 17, 1860, after a three-year retirement, financial difficulties forced Forrest back on stage, with the seats sold at auction for opening night.[117]

During Forrest's absence from the New York stage, Edwin Booth had emerged as America's preeminent Shakespearean tragedian, adding a subtlety and sense of movement far different from Forrest's staid declamatory demeanor. A new, intense rivalry was in the wings. Booth's threatening presence in town was supplemented by that of Charlotte Cushman, who had become Forrest's bitter enemy during the early years of his rivalry with William Macready, as well as during his 1845 tour of England when he was booed and she was applauded over and over.

Forrest deliberately chose Niblo's giant auditorium as the largest establishment available, and stayed there for six months. His contract required three performances each week, and it was left to the producer to fill the house with other shows on Forrest's nights off. Opera was chosen, and ticket prices were increased for the musical offerings, as they tended to attract a wealthier crowd than Forrest's traditional fan base. Forrest's performances were critically acclaimed, though, with even the staid *Times* complimenting his talents.[118]

FIGURE 44: *Grand Masquerade Ball of the Arion Society, At Niblo's Theatre New York, February 11; from* Frank Leslie's Illustrated Newspaper *Mar. 7, 1863, pg. 372; Collection of The New-York Historical Society*

A few months before Forrest's return to the stage, strange visitors were seen promenading around the outdoor sections of Niblo's Garden. With the dawn of American-Japanese diplomatic and trade relations, an Imperial delegation arrived in the United States in May 1860, the first group of citizens from that country ever to visit American shores. Underwritten with copious amounts of U.S. government funds, the visit was questioned severely by some citizens as imprudent, and the pageants and parades as "contemptible absurdities."[119] The group's arrival in New York on June 16 was the cause of much celebration, though, with parades and dinners sponsored by the city. The contingent set up their base in the Metropolitan Hotel, and made it their practice to stroll through the interior courtyard as well as the streets of New York in traditional formal dress, astonishing other guests and passersby.

The City Council decided to sponsor a ball in honor of the delegation, and Niblo's Garden, with its gigantic opera house, separate saloon, and ballroom, was chosen as the optimal venue. On Monday, June 25, 12,000 guests attended the festivities, which the *Times* proclaimed the next morning a "grand festival, which all night long thundered with carriages and lightened with gas lamps."[120] Niblo's reputation as leader of municipal entertainment was permanently sealed.

The Japanese Ball and Edwin Forrest's triumphant return to his Bowery B'hoy-filled audiences at Niblo's Garden marked the last year of Niblo's active involvement in the stage. At the end of April 1861, Niblo's Garden closed for extensive renovations after his lease came to an end, and the property was taken over by merchant prince Alexander T. Stewart. Though his name would shine from the Broadway signage for decades thereafter, Niblo, age 71, bid adieu to the theater world he had dominated for 33 years, and he turned his attentions to overseas travel, philanthropy, and an already deep involvement in the affairs of Gramercy Park's Calvary Episcopal Church.[121]

Chapter 5
CALVARY CHURCH

~~~~~~

Though he had had married in his wife's family's First Presbyterian Church on Wall Street, and was likely raised as a Presbyterian, Niblo did not become a member of that parish. Niblo's mother, Mary, likely was. She died in 1825, and was buried in First Presbyterian's Forsyth Street cemetery after her funeral was conducted from the Bank Coffee House.[122] American Protestants with social and commercial aspirations frequently "moved up" by joining an Episcopalian parish, and Niblo followed that path.

Niblo's religious faith extended well beyond attendance at church. The American Bible Society listed him as a donor as early as 1817, and by 1828, Niblo was a subscriber to the Society for the Encouragement of Faithful Domestic Servants. Its purposes were to encourage "perfect moral behavior" and religious faith in household staff, chiefly young women. Subscribers were encouraged to register their servants above 15 years of age with the Society, and if at the end of a year, their conduct was flawless, servants would be rewarded with "a handsome Bible . . . or three volumes of Tracts." Annual cash rewards were offered to each such servant who continued in the employ of the subscriber and behaved perfectly, totaling $40 over seven years maximum. The prize tracts included Benjamin Franklin's *Poor Richard*, and two by unidentified authors entitled *A Father's Advice to his Daughter on going out to Service*, and *Sarah, or the Victim of Pride*. The society grew out of a similar effort in London, and was closely involved with the workings of the New York Female Tract Society.[123] Subscribers to the New York Society included members of the Auchincloss, Chesebrough, Delafield, Fish, Hone, Roosevelt, Schermerhorn, and Stuyvesant families, as well as abolitionist Arthur Tappan and Niblo's business associate Ramsay Crooks.

Niblo's beneficent attitude toward domestic servants did not match up with his morals about human slavery, though. New York State passed a gradual abolition act in 1799, but Niblo continued to own a slave named Henry Davis until 1817. A further abolition act became law that year, but it is unclear whether it or the prior law required Niblo to free his slave. Total emancipation became effective in 1827.[124]

After a relationship with St. Thomas Episcopal Church in lower Manhattan, the parish church that was to win Niblo's long-term allegiance was a newly formed one in New York. Calvary Episcopal was founded in 1835 by a group of Episcopalians that included Columbia College professor John McVickar (also Vice-President of the New York Protestant Episcopal City Mission Society), merchant Henry Seaman, and attorneys Frederic de Peyster and J. Rutsen Van Rensselaer, Jr. A plot of land was leased on Fourth Avenue (now Park Avenue South) near 30th Street (as yet unopened), and a clapboard structure was erected, one of the first churches in the city north of 14th Street and south of 34th Street. Uptown villages such as Bloomingdale on what is now called the Upper West Side, Manhattanville (centering on 125th Street and Amsterdam Avenue), and Harlem boasted a variety of houses of Christian worship, but the blocks around the new Calvary Church were destitute of such structures.[125]

Calvary was founded with missionary purposes, and intimately connected with a Sunday School founded in the early 1830s by Professor McVickar and students at the General Theological Seminary, which was located near the present-day site of the church at 21st Street and Park Avenue South. McVickar, credited with being the true father of Calvary, was an ordained Episcopal minister, and taught moral and intellectual philosophy, rhetoric, belles lettres, and political economy at Columbia.[126]

The environs of the new church were sparsely populated, and the newly laid tracks of the New York and Harlem Railroad ran right by the front door, at grade level. Coal cinders and smoke undoubtedly coated the frocks and coats of parishioners as the carriages rattled by. Two blocks north sat Sunfish Pond, fed by a stream flowing south from 44th Street and known for its rich stock of eels. The pond was not drained and filled in until 1839. Peter Cooper's glue factory also graced the immediate neighborhood. Sunday School and religious services commenced in the half-completed structure in April 1836 under the supervision of an unordained minister, General Theological Seminary student Thomas

Dupont. By December, the little frame church was completed and furnished with pews from St. Mark's Parish. The green-painted building measured 46 feet by 29 feet and was designed to move easily off its foundation to a new site.

The rapid development of the neighborhoods south of the original Calvary site and the upward mobility of the residents attracted to Union Square, Irving Place, and Gramercy Park significantly impacted the organization, membership, and control of Calvary toward the end of its first decade. Legally incorporated on October 5, 1836, Calvary struggled financially during its early years, sometimes pleading with Trinity Parish for essential financial support. The Panic of 1837 came woefully early in the new church's life, and only by dint of Trinity's support was Calvary able to survive. Its original vision of being a "free" church, without pew sales or rentals, grew dim, even while the Sunday School grew by leaps and bounds.

Men of strong religious beliefs formed Calvary, and Niblo numbered among the earliest members of the church and supporters of its missionary activities to the poor, which figured greatly in the founders' intentions. Niblo joined the Board of the Domestic and Foreign Missionary Society in 1839 and later served as a vestryman and as a warden during the last decade of his life. When Niblo had opened his Garden in 1828, replacing the stables at the site, he likely became acquainted with Archibald Gracie, Jr., among those who kept horses there or nearby. Gracie, his brother Robert, and his father, Archibald, Sr., became supporters of Calvary Parish in the earliest years of Niblo's involvement with it.

Calvary's lease of its original sanctuary site was scheduled to expire in 1840, and many parishioners were averse to renewing it because of the clatter of railroad cars and milkmen's wagons on Fourth Avenue, as well as the tight fit of a growing congregation in the small structure. The landlord offered five more years with an option for the tenant to cancel at the end of any lease year, so Calvary stayed put while a new site was sought. A lot on the northeast corner of Fourth Avenue and 22nd Street became available for purchase upon favorable terms from the merchant Philip Kearny. By the end of 1841, the old lease was canceled, the lot eight blocks south purchased, and arrangements made to move the clapboard chapel downtown, leaving only the foundation (excluding its window sashes, doors, and frames) as a cancellation payment to the lessor. The purchase of the lots brought the wealthy and well-connected Kearny brothers into the parish, and the moving of the structure was paid for by subscribers including Samuel Ruggles, Peter Cooper (whose residence was nearby at Lexington Avenue and 22nd Street), and Thomas Addis Emmet (a well-known jurist and Irish patriot). Signatures with surnames such as Chesebrough, Pyne, and Charles King (then president of Columbia College) rounded out the list of socially prominent supporters, though not necessarily parishioners, who made the move possible.

The little wooden structure was expanded after the move to accommodate an almost threefold increase in pews, but finances continued to be difficult and the support of Trinity Parish essential. Gramercy Park developer Samuel Ruggles joined the parish in the early 1840s as his most famous development took shape nearby, and in 1844, perhaps the best-known nineteenth-century pastor of Calvary was hired, cleric Samuel Lewis Southard. The growth of the congregation and the surrounding neighborhood's development as a center of residences for the upper middle class dictated the construction of an entirely new building. Having determined that the 22nd Street site might be unsuitable for the foundation of a larger stone structure, the parish acquired lots on the next block south, literally across the street from Gramercy Park, and hired 25-year-old James Renwick, Jr., to design a magnificent addition to his portfolio of work. Renwick had recently served as the Superintendent of Construction of the Demotic-styled Croton Receiving Reservoir on the west side of Fifth Avenue between 40th and 42nd Streets, and his lacy Gothic Grace Church was nearing completion on Broadway at Tenth Street.[127] The cornerstone for Calvary was laid on March 3, 1846, and the building was consecrated on June 4, 1847. Gifts of Communion silver came from the Kearny family, whose most famous member had been a founder of the New York Stock Exchange thirty years earlier.

Reverend Southard's prominence as a cleric, coupled with the church's ideal location, continued to attract new parishioners of social and financial means: attorney Ogden Hoffman and controversial newspaper publisher James Watson Webb joined in the late 1840s. The names were topped, perhaps, by the celebration of the wedding of John Jacob Astor, Jr., to Charlotte Augusta Gibbes by Reverend Southard on December 9, 1846. George Templeton Strong and Joseph Beers (a close friend of the well-known New York Episcopalian cleric Rev. Francis Lister Hawks) joined the Vestry of Calvary by 1849, but financial difficulties continued and finally led to Reverend Southard's resignation in 1849. Southard was followed by Rev. Jonathan M. Wainwright, but he resigned the next year.

Calvary parishioners were fortunate with their choice of Rev. Francis Lister Hawks as the next leader of the parish, a post he held for twelve years beginning in 1850. Hawks had had a distinguished if checkered career in New York since 1831 in his leadership of two downtown churches, St. Stephen's and then St. Thomas's. His sermons at the former attracted large crowds, and many parishioners followed him to St. Thomas's when it lured him away only nine months after he joined St. Stephen's. A blackface minstrel performer, George Washington Dixon, accused Hawks of sexual improprieties during the seventh year of his tenure at St. Thomas's, and although Dixon lost a libel suit brought by the cleric, the charges were well publicized and haunted Hawks for years thereafter.

Hawks was also well acquainted with Niblo, a St. Thomas's parishioner in the early 1840s. Hawks resigned his post at St. Thomas's in late October 1843 and was brought up on charges at the General Convention of 1844 in Philadelphia, accused of having a "malicious disposition" and "a licentious tongue." Dixon's scandalous claims as well as the controversy surrounding Hawks's alleged financial mismanagement of the St. Thomas Hall boys' school in Flushing, which failed in 1842 within its third year of operation, most likely informed the Convention charges. Niblo's signature appears on a document dated October 11, 1844, as one of many men who state themselves to have been acquainted with Hawks for at least twelve years and are members of St. Thomas's. The men provided a vigorous testament to Hawks's morality and strength of character.[128]

After his resignation from St. Thomas's, Reverend Hawks moved to a post in Mississippi and then to Christ Church in New Orleans, where he served from 1847 to 1849 as the first president of what is now Tulane University. During Hawks's absence from New York, Niblo strengthened his involvement in the affairs of Calvary Church, and supported the May

16, 1850, call from the Vestry Committee to Reverend Hawks to lead the congregation. Hawks had returned from the South to New York to serve as pastor of the Church of the Mediator on Eighth Street near Fourth Avenue, and after lengthy negotiations, a merger of the two churches was arranged. Hawks moved uptown to lead Calvary, accepting an employment contract at an annual salary of $5,000 as of June 26.

A charismatic speaker and well-respected historiographer of the Episcopal Church in America, Hawks was selected by the Vestry of Calvary, among other reasons, to lead the campaign to stabilize the chronically underfinanced parish. The congregation implemented a recapitalization based on pew sales that would wipe out its financial problems. All pew holders were required to return their titles to the parish in exchange for scrip, and then rebid for their pews in an auction. The results were a blessing for the parish, and in 1850 a new pew seating plan and list were promulgated.

Pew #113, on the left of the center aisle, third row in from the altar and pulpit, was acquired for $650 by Niblo in the sale on Wednesday, October 9, 1850. The price was the highest fixed for a similar-size pew. Among the other purchasers were Robert Gracie, John J. Astor, Jr., William Beekman, Richard L. Schiefflin, and a host of other well-known New York society names. A peculiar entry is for pew #136: "F.L. Hawks – McReady" is entered as the purchaser in church records. Why the pastor acquired a pew, and to whom "McReady" refers, are unknown. Two hundred sixty-four pews were sold off at prices ranging from $700 for a double-sized pew immediately by the steps leading up to altar, down to $70 far in the back of the sanctuary.

Funds became available to pay off all parish debts, install gas lines around the chancel, pulpit, and desk, repair the chancel windows, repurchase the original Rectory structure (which had been deeded to the builder in 1848 to secure the Church's promise to pay for completion, and leased back when the congregation ran short of funds), and purchase the lot on the north side of the church on Fourth Avenue. The parish's Benevolent Society flourished with the new fiscal stability, and a women's committee, headed by Mrs. Hawks and including Mrs. John Jacob Astor as well as Mrs. Richard Delafield and Mrs. J. Van Rensselear, conducted a fund-raising campaign that paid poor seamstresses to sew

9,900 garments for Calvary Sunday School children in 1851.[129]

Reverend Hawks's tenure also brought Calvary a new reputation for high-quality musical performance when it hired Henry Wellington Greatorex, whose about-to-be-published *Collection of Psalm and Hymn Tunes* (Boston, 1851) quickly became well known as *The Greatorex Collection*. His hymnal was used in many Protestant denominations for decades thereafter. The highlight of 1850 at Calvary was a concert by Jenny Lind, whose tour of America under the sponsorship of P. T. Barnum began in September of that year.

Reverend Hawks's advocacy of missionary activities by the Calvary parish was energetic, and brought a marked increase in fund-raising earmarked for the Domestic and Foreign Missionary Society, which had been founded in the early years of Calvary's existence. Established to serve an "unchurched" area of the sparsely populated east side, the sanctuary saw the makeup of its worshippers change drastically when financial problems necessitated the sale of pews, described above, in which only those wealthy enough to purchase or rent could sit. Hawks called a meeting on the day after Christmas 1856 to address the inequality problem and forthwith founded a separate Missionary Association "for the purpose of providing for the physical and spiritual destitution of the Poor in that portion of the City of New York immediately adjacent to Calvary church."[130]

FIGURE 45: *Reverend Francis Lister Hawks.*

The large lecture room of the Columbia College of Physicians and Surgeons, recently erected on 23rd Street and Fourth Avenue, was rented for one year. By the following year, 152 families were being served by the Mission, and the congregation acquired lots on 23rd Street between Second and Third Avenues where, in 1860, the 23rd Street Chapel opened its doors. The building promptly burned down, and was reopened in a new structure on the same site in October 1861. Niblo was instrumental in the formation and erection of the 23rd Street Chapel, and a significant donor to it.[131]

In the later part of 1860, Reverend Hawks received an urgent request from an Irish woman named Eliza Gilbert. Better known to the world as the infamous Lola Montez, the supplicant had been smitten on June 30 with paralysis on her left side, a most unfortunate occurrence for a performer, courtesan, and author who was politely described by one contemporary memoirist as "a danseuse of considerable and various fame, who appealed rather to nature than to the artistic sense."[132] Niblo was instrumental in the acquaintance between Montez and Reverend Hawks.

Hawks visited Montez for many months, always in the company of Maria Buchanan, Montez's childhood friend and nurse, deeming it his duty, as he wrote in the parish records, "to bear witness to the 'mighty power of the Holy Ghost' in changing the heart of one who had been a great sinner." Hawks was deeply impressed with Montez's humility and desire to reform as well as her interest in reading scripture for herself. On his first visit, Hawks claimed that when he took up the Bible from a table, it opened of its own accord to the story of Christ forgiving the Magdalen in the house of Simon. He listened to Montez "with admiration, as with the tears streaming from her eyes, her right [unparalyzed] hand uplifted, and her singularly expressive features (her keen black eye especially) speaking almost as plainly as her tongue, she would dwell upon Christ and the almost incredible truth that He could show mercy to such a vile sinner as she felt herself to have been."[133] Reverend Hawks's ministry to Montez apparently brought her substantial relief: the former mistress of King Ludwig I of Bavaria recovered enough mobility by mid-December to stroll outside

FIGURE 46: *Lola Montez.*

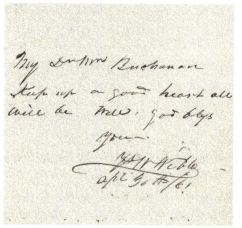

FIGURE 47: *Letter from William Niblo to Maria Buchanan, April ___, 1861; Courtesy of Harvard Theatre Collection, Houghton Library, Harvard University.*

in cold weather. She contracted pneumonia, though, lingered for a month, and died on January 17, 1861, at age forty, with Reverend Hawks at her side.[134] Niblo's written condolences were sent to Buchanan later that year, after Montez was laid to rest not far from the Niblo mausoleum at Green-Wood Cemetery.

Reverend Hawks's tenure at Calvary ended on a bad note when, as a Southern sympathizer, he refused to fly the Union flag over the church at the outbreak of the Civil War. A mob gathered and threatened to burn the building down, and when the sexton rushed to Hawks with the news, the flag was hoisted and the church saved. The official correspondence concerning resignation of his pulpit in the spring of 1862 made no mention of the dispute, and the vestry reluctantly accepted his departure in April. After a brief clerical appointment in Baltimore, Hawks returned to New York, but passed away on September 26, 1866. On the same day, the Chapel of the Holy Saviour organized by Niblo and John Alstyne on 25th Street was accepted into the Episcopal Convention.[135]

Hawks's death must have been devastating for Niblo. Though no correspondence appears to have survived, the strength of their bond is clear: Hawks's considerable library of American history ended up at the New-York Historical Society through Niblo's good offices. Hawks was a steadfast supporter of the Society, and upon his death, Niblo purchased hundreds of Hawks's books from his estate and then donated the collection to the Society.[136] An ornate tribute to Hawks from his spiritual friend adorns the north wall of the nave of Calvary Church. In 1873, a magnificent stained glass window was installed "In Memory of Rev. F.L. Hawks, D.D., LL.D., by his friend, Wm Niblo."

FIGURE 48: *Stained Glass Window at Calvary Episcopal Church, New York City, dedicated to Rev. Francis Lister Hawks by William Niblo (author photo).*

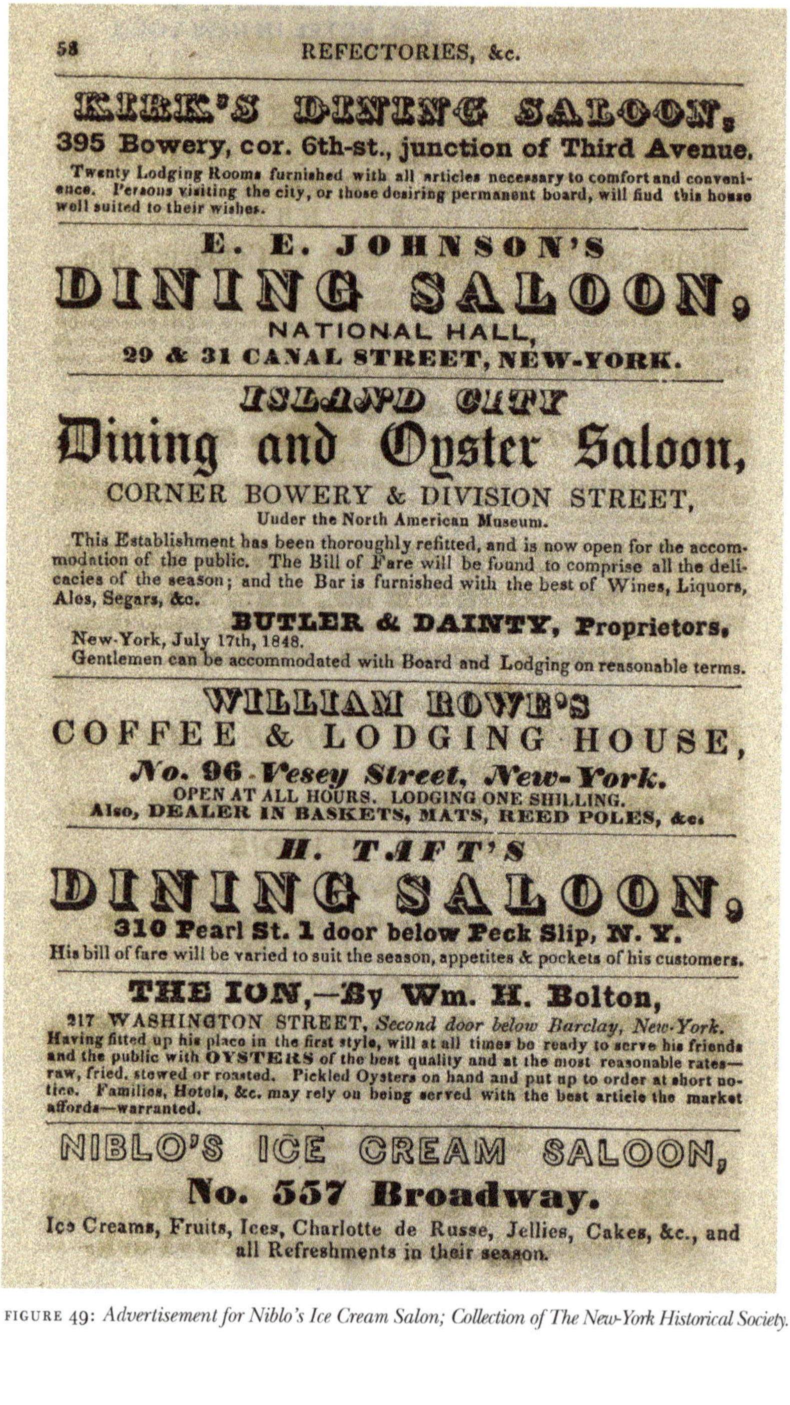

KIRK'S DINING SALOON,
395 Bowery, cor. 6th-st., junction of Third Avenue.

Twenty Lodging Rooms furnished with all articles necessary to comfort and convenience. Persons visiting the city, or those desiring permanent board, will find this house well suited to their wishes.

E. E. JOHNSON'S
DINING SALOON,
NATIONAL HALL,
29 & 31 CANAL STREET, NEW-YORK.

ISLAND CITY
Dining and Oyster Saloon,
CORNER BOWERY & DIVISION STREET,
Under the North American Museum.

This Establishment has been thoroughly refitted, and is now open for the accommodation of the public. The Bill of Fare will be found to comprise all the delicacies of the season; and the Bar is furnished with the best of Wines, Liquors, Ales, Segars, &c.

BUTLER & DAINTY, Proprietors.
New-York, July 17th, 1848.
Gentlemen can be accommodated with Board and Lodging on reasonable terms.

WILLIAM ROWE'S
COFFEE & LODGING HOUSE,
No. 96 Vesey Street, New-York.
OPEN AT ALL HOURS. LODGING ONE SHILLING.
Also, DEALER IN BASKETS, MATS, REED POLES, &c.

H. TAFT'S
DINING SALOON,
310 Pearl St. 1 door below Peck Slip, N. Y.

His bill of fare will be varied to suit the season, appetites & pockets of his customers.

THE ION,—By Wm. H. Bolton,

217 WASHINGTON STREET, *Second door below Barclay, New-York.* Having fitted up his place in the first style, will at all times be ready to serve his friends and the public with OYSTERS of the best quality and at the most reasonable rates—raw, fried, stewed or roasted. Pickled Oysters on hand and put up to order at short notice. Families, Hotels, &c. may rely on being served with the best article the market affords—warranted.

NIBLO'S ICE CREAM SALOON,
No. 557 Broadway.

Ice Creams, Fruits, Ices, Charlotte de Russe, Jellies, Cakes, &c., and all Refreshments in their season.

FIGURE 49: *Advertisement for Niblo's Ice Cream Salon; Collection of The New-York Historical Society.*

Chapter 6
NIBLO'S EMPIRE

While in command of what must have been substantial positive cash flow from the opening of the Bank Coffee House in 1813 until his 1861 retirement from an active role in managing his pleasure garden, Niblo engaged in a multitude of business ventures, including loaning money and accepting promissory notes. He frequently resorted to litigation to collect upon them when the obligors defaulted. His real estate investments extended over a wide swath of Manhattan south of 96th Street.

Niblo's success in business was certainly in part attributable to his jovial manner and modest, sober disposition. Help from his brother John, five years his senior, was likely also important as William built his empire. By 1820, John had settled in Petersburg, Virginia, where he operated a tavern until it burned in 1827. He built the Bollingbrook Hotel in Petersburg a year later. In 1830, John was operating the City Hotel at 41 North Third Street in Philadelphia with a partner. By the fall of 1832, John made his way to New York City, where he took over the National Hotel at 112 Broadway and renamed it the Congress Hall. John is listed in New York City directories as having run a coffee house at 157 Broadway in the mid-1830s while living on lower Eighth Avenue. For many years thereafter, his business address was at William's establishment at 576 Broadway, while he resided in Spring Street. In the mid-1840s, John operated a florist business at Niblo's Garden, and during those years moved to 413 and then 537 Houston Street. An 1852 display ad in the *American Advertiser* solicits customers for "Niblo's Ice Cream Saloon" at 557 Broadway, one block south and across the street from the Broadway entrance to Niblo's Garden and the new Metropolitan Hotel. John was the operator of this parlor, and it undoubtedly benefited from its proximity to the larger establishments one block uptown.

John operated the Congress Hall Hotel for an extended period, and lived on Houston Street for many years with his wife Eliza and their daughters. Eliza died in 1859 of a gangrenous lump and was interred in Green-Wood Cemetery in John's vault, which sits on the hilltop above William's mausoleum. Shortly thereafter, John moved in with his daughter Martha Sloat and her husband John in Norwalk, Connecticut. He lived for six more years. The certificate of his death on July 16, 1866, records his residence as Hollyroad Place in the 19th Ward in New York and his occupation as wine merchant.[137]

Despite his successes with the Bank Coffee House and Niblo's Garden, it seems that William Niblo never amassed a gigantic fortune, whether due to his philanthropic activities or the vagaries of business. His real and personal property was valued in 1822 by municipal authorities at a total of $17,400, when the Bank Coffee House was at its apex. Twenty-eight years later, with the newly reconstructed Garden open for one year, his real estate was valued at $132,400.[138]

Dozens of cases with Niblo's name as either plaintiff or defendant fill the indices of the New York City Court of Common Pleas, Chancery Court, and Supreme Court. Several concern alleged unpaid rent on Niblo's Garden by promoters who rented the premises for various productions. There are also claims against Niblo for unpaid compensation by performers at Niblo's Garden. A few concern disputes with employees at the original Bank Coffee House, but the bulk of the lawsuits are attempts by Niblo to collect on short-term instruments he accepted as security for repayment of small loans extended to individuals for unspecified purposes. Niblo was frequently sued for unpaid monies for various reasons, and apparently was skillful at evading collection when he lost.[139]

One of Niblo's long-time business associates was the fur trader Ramsay Crooks, whose successful career in the early decades of the nineteenth century in upstate New York and the Midwest propelled him into the upper middle class in New York. There, Crooks established himself as a "general commission merchant" in various Wall Street and City Hall offices. Crooks engaged in several transactions with Niblo in the early 1830s, conveying a great deal of personal property in the small buildings leased by Niblo from Crooks at Broadway and Prince Streets. Crooks also loaned Niblo cash, the alleged nonpayment of which was disputed and led to litigation.[140] The men must have made up their quarrels in later years: Crooks was temporarily interred in the Niblo mausoleum for four years after his death in June 1859.

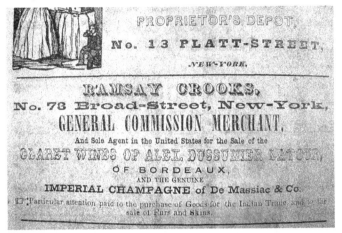

FIGURE 50: Ramsay Crooks Display Advertisement in Longworth's New York Directory c. 1850.

Niblo was known throughout his career as a gentleman and a keeper of marital vows. His career as a respecter of womanhood came forth in an unusual piece of litigation brought by him in 1846 as the procedurally required "next friend" of Jane Walmsley, a married woman seeking a divorce from her abusive husband.[141]

In September 1846, Niblo agreed to plead in Chancery Court as next friend of Jane, who had married Thomas M. in 1824 and lived with him for 22 years. Thomas was a printer, and the couple had lived on Laurens, Ferry, Wooster, Spring, and Lumber Streets through 1835 but then disappear from New York City directories for ten years. Jane herself reappears in 1846, living at 60 Stanton Street, without Thomas. Jane bore him six children, three of whom survived at the date of the divorce complaint. Alleging cruel and inhuman treatment over a long period, Jane swore that Thomas had, on July 3, struck her without provocation, causing massive bleeding from the face, and then struck her so hard that she had to grab the stair bannister so as not to fall down. Jane's husband was said to have dragged her down the stairs into the yard, beating her in front of their son, Thomas, Jr., and then locking the two of them back up in the house, where he continued to beat both of them cruelly. Mrs. Walmsley sought

85

shelter from municipal authorities on that occasion, and also complained of a ten-year period of cruel violence and of having fed and educated her children unassisted by her husband. Jane said she was often compelled to walk the streets through the night with an infant in her arms when Thomas would rage and lock her out of the house.

The signature page of Walmsley's complaint for divorce and prayer for custody by Niblo's "friend," an illiterate woman, was signed by Niblo, with an X to indicate her authorization. How Niblo became acquainted with Jane Walmsley remains unclear: neither her name nor her husband's appears in the extant registers of members of Calvary Church, nor can any connections be deduced from census, address directory, or other sources. Niblo's leadership of the 23rd Street Chapel of Calvary Church perhaps put him in contact with more than one such miserable life. The outcome of the case is also unknown.

Although Niblo operated the Bank Coffee House on Pine Street and Niblo's Garden on leased property, he was an active investor in real estate in other parts of Manhattan, including his country house in the exurban reaches of Yorkville near present-day 86th Street and the East River. The Niblos' uptown home was one of the sort described by Alexis de Tocqueville in a letter to his mother from May 14, 1831, as his ship entered Hell-Gate from the Long Island Sound, along "a lovely sweep of notched shoreline, blossoming trees on greensward sloping down to the water, a multitude of small, artfully embellished candy-box houses in the background."[142]

Though platted on the 1818 Commissioners' Map of Manhattan, the streets between 79th Street and 96th Street running east of Third Avenue were mostly unopened through the 1840s, with large holdings of men such as John Jacob Astor dominating the East River waterfront in the area of what is now Carl Schurz Park (84th Street to 92nd Street, east of East End Avenue).

York Avenue (so named in 1928 in honor of First World War hero Sgt. Alvin York) and East End Avenue were platted as northerly extensions of Avenues A and B, respectively, and also remained largely paper streets through much of the nineteenth century. Country lanes led down to the waterfront where ferries took travelers to Hallet's Point in what is now Queens County as well as other points north and east. Regardless of the absence of passable thoroughfares, much of the neighborhood was carved up and sold off as investor lots, and Niblo was an active purchaser. The majority of his acquisitions in the mid-1840s (before Martha Niblo's death) consisted of lots on 83rd and 84th Streets between Avenues A and B. It is likely that the agglomeration formed the country estate whose development Martha superintended. Other purchases on 86th, 88th, and 89th Streets near Avenue B came after her death.[143]

In addition to Niblo's ardent support of Calvary Church, his philanthropy extended to the American Bible Society, the Young Men's Christian Association, and the National Academy of Design. In 1859, Niblo purchased four lots at the southwest corner of 23rd Street and Fourth Avenue from J. Watts and Estelle de Peyster (a member of a prominent Cal-

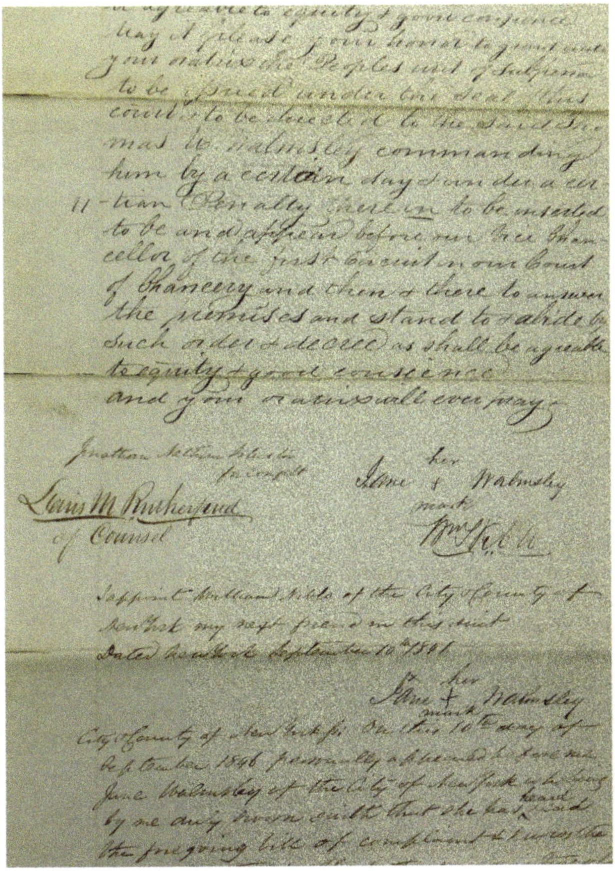
agreeable to equity & good conscience
May it please your honor to grant unto
your oratrix the People's writ of subpoena
to be issued under the seal of this
court to be directed to the said Thomas W. Walmsley commanding
him by a certain day & under a certain Penalty therein to be inserted
to be and appear before our Vice Chan-
cellor of the first Circuit in our Court
of Chancery and then & there to answer
the premises and stand to & abide by
such order & decree as shall be agreeable
to equity & good conscience
and your oratrix shall ever pray &c

Jane her + mark Walmsley

Louis M. Rutherfurd
of Counsel

Wm. Niblo

I appoint William Niblo of the City & County of
New York my next friend in this suit
Dated New York September 10th 1846

Jane her + mark Walmsley

City & County of New York ss: On this 10th day of
September 1846 personally appeared before me
Jane Walmsley of the City of New York ...
by me duly sworn saith that she has heard read
the foregoing bill of complaint ...

FIGURE 51: *Walmsley Divorce Complaint.*

vary Church family). Two years later, Niblo (who was also a cash donor to the Academy) conveyed the lots to Asher Durand and the other Trustees of the Academy. Durand, along with Samuel F. B. Morse and other prominent young graphic artists, formed an association in 1825 as a rebellious offshoot from the stodgy American Academy of the Fine Arts.[144] A magnificent palazzo-style headquarters was erected on site. It served for many years as the home of the National Academy until the institution moved to the southern edge of Morningside Heights and then to its present home on Fifth Avenue. (The 23rd Street façade was carefully deconstructed when that building was demolished in 1890 and reinstalled as part of the façade of Our Lady of Lourdes on West 142nd Street.)[145]

Niblo's residences after years of living on the grounds of his pleasure garden included a house constructed by him on the southeast corner of 20th Street and Bloomingdale Road. His neighbors on the block included Cornelius Roosevelt, Silas Weir, Peter Goelet (one of New York's wealthiest citizens), and Samuel Ruggles. Niblo's first purchase on the block was in 1841, and in 1843 Niblo successfully negotiated with Goelet to build a gable on Niblo's house that encroached on Goelet's property. Though no photo of the Niblo mansion survives, one of Goelet's does:

FIGURE 52:
Peter Goelet house, c. *1915, from* Henry Collins Brown, New York of To-day *(New York: The Old Colony Press, 1917).*

FIGURE 53: *National Academy of Design, 4th Avenue and 23rd Street, from Henry Collins Brown,* New York of To-day *(New York: The Old Colony Press, 1917).*

FIGURE 54: *Our Lady of Lourdes, 472 West 142nd Street (author photo).*

Niblo also acquired property on the southeast corner of Broadway and Eighth Street, and on the south side of Ninth Street, west of Broadway, as well as parcels on 29th Street and 23rd Street, both between Second and Third Avenues (the latter two parcels were, perhaps, connected with Niblo's efforts on behalf of missions of Calvary Church). Municipal records indicate that after his wife's untimely death in 1851, Niblo lived on the Crosby Street side of his Garden at number 121, where his neighbors were shopkeepers, Contoit's Stables, a lamp dealer named Joseph Stourenel, and a billiards merchant named Abraham Bassford.[146]

FIGURE 55: *Crosby Street side of Niblo's Garden c. 1835, Courtesy of The New York Public Library Digital Images Collections.*

Chapter 7
A DIGNIFIED END

A̲fter more than fifty years spent in the public eye as a tavernkeep, theater owner, and impresario, Niblo may well have found retirement a pleasant change from the hubbub of civic life. Still vigorous beyond 70, Niblo kept busy with involvement in Christian affairs of many kinds, his wide group of club friends, and extensive foreign travel, even though his name gradually lost its fame in the city's entertainment world. Litigation records also evidence his ongoing involvement in lending money for short terms to various recalcitrant individuals, as well as a still-active career as a real estate investor in New York.

On December 31, 1852, not even a year after losing his wife, Niblo paid $300 apiece for lots 6618-6625 at Green-Wood Cemetery, assuring himself a sizable site adjacent to tranquil Crescent Water upon which to build a family mausoleum. On July 13, 1854, Martha King Niblo (who had passed away on February 11, 1851, and was interred in lot 4264 at Green-Wood) and her mother, Catherine King (who outlived her daughter by only five and a half months and was interred in her daughter's lot) were entombed in a magnificent stone structure, whose portal is guarded by two stately lions. The Niblo mausoleum also holds the remains of Niblo's mother, Mary Niblo, and Martha's father, David King, both placed there on July 18, 1854.

It is unknown whether any of Niblo's guests at his frequent picnics at the mausoleum ever commented among themselves or to their host on the beautiful sculpture of a dormant, recumbent youth that was installed in the mausoleum in 1855. The circumstances of its installation and the identity of the little boy were lost to time after Niblo's passing in 1878, and the extensive records of the cemetery contain no information about it. Though one account asserts that the Niblos had at least one child, the ledgers of the New York City Almshouse tell a different tale.[147]

On October 16, 1818, with a check from N. Jarvis for $300, Niblo posted a bastardy bond with the New York City Almshouse, then located on Blackwell's Island, for the care of William Henry Niblo, a boy born two years and four days before. The boy's mother, Sarah Jane Hannan, collected over $171 in "lying in expenses" from the bond until September 1, 1820. The first $50 was paid to Sarah on the boy's second birthday. Periodic payments thereafter perhaps reimbursed Sarah for outlays to one or more nurses who cared for the child: the caption in the ledger mentions the boy being "at nurse with ____Thompson No. ____ Reade Street at ___ per month." Irregular payments of up to $17.50 were made to Sarah until September 1, 1820. "N. Jarvis" is almost certainly Noah Jarvis, an acquaintance of and cocontributor with Niblo to the American Bible Society in 1817, as well as Collector of Assessments for the City of New York from 1811 to 1828 and manager of the estate of Stephen Van Rensselaer, from whom Niblo leased the site of Niblo's Garden in later years.[148]

Poverty and the shame of illegitimacy created a tidal flow of foundlings in New York City, and though William Henry Niblo was not a foundling, his fate probably did not differ from the other young inmates at the Almshouse. Niblo's son was admitted to the Almshouse on October 6, 1818, where adults and children lived in common quarters.[149] The boy appeared in the 1818 and 1822 censuses of Almshouse inmates. The next extant census ledger is dated 1834, when the boy would have turned 18. Even if he survived to this ripe age, he would not have still lived in the Almshouse, so his absence from the 1834 ledger is inconclusive as to his longevity. Almshouse children as young as seven were sent out to labor in homes and factories in frequently abysmal conditions. Mortality rates for Almshouse children were extremely high, and William, Jr., probably did not survive into adulthood. His father may well have been apprised of his death, suffering silently with the knowledge and guilt until and even after his wife died in 1851.

Whether Martha King Niblo was ever told of her husband's premarital indiscretion will never be known. William Niblo was likely acquainted with Martha when Sarah Hannan became pregnant by him in early 1816, because Niblo had worked for Martha's father more than three years earlier. A devout Christian, Niblo may have hidden his shame about his youthful sin from his dearly beloved for their entire acquaintance and lives together. The sculpture was created four years after Martha's death.

During the last year of his life, Niblo took up lodging at 10 East 24th Street with Mary Sylvester, who, due to Niblo's infirmity, had verified Niblo's signature on his contract to acquire the house for $32,500 in March.[150] The house was purchased by Niblo for Sylvester, and he moved there from his prior lodgings at 50 West 28th Street some time before the April 4, 1878, codicil to his will (executed three years prior). In that codicil, which the testator executed with a shaky "X" as his mark, a prior bequest of $30,000 to Mary was revoked, in consideration of the fact that Niblo had given her the $32,500 necessary to acquire 10 East 24th Street and take title thereto.[151] Mary is described in Niblo's will as his "faithful servant and nurse," and the bequest is made on account of her service to Niblo and his late wife.

FIGURE 56: *Inside the Niblo Mausoleum at Green-Wood Cemetery; photo by Jeffrey Richman, Resident Historian.*

FIGURE 57: *The underside of the baby sculpture: Inside the Niblo Mausoleum at Green-Wood Cemetery, photo by Jeffrey Richman, Resident Historian.*

It was the frail old man's custom toward the end of his life to place a bell upon his bed-stand in order to summon help if necessary. In the middle of one August night, Niblo awoke, rose, and suddenly felt powerless and speechless. Able only to crawl toward the little table, he grasped the cloth cover and pulled it off, carrying the bell with it. Mary Sylvester heard the tinkle and rushed into the room, only to hear Niblo indistinctly speak his characteristically droll last words: "Ah, Mary, floored at last . . . ." The paralyzing stroke proved a death sentence for the once virile man.[152] Niblo passed away on the morning of August 21, 1878.

On Saturday morning, August 24, 1878, four men bore a solid oak casket fitted with heavy silver ornaments and covered with a black velvet cloth to the altar of Calvary Church. A silver plate on the casket bore the inscription *WILLIAM NIBLO Born Aug. 1, 1790 Died Aug. 21, 1878.* Adjacent to the shining nameplate lay a miniature sheaf of wheat and a wreath of palm, which, at the request of family members, were the only botanical tributes contributed to the sad proceedings. Though Niblo seems to have had no issue except the illegitimate son he sired by Sarah Hannan (the son likely having died before having issue of his own), a snowy pillow bearing the word "Grandpa" decorated the scene. Niblo's two young nieces, daughters of his brother John, followed the coffin to the front of the sanctuary.

A brief service followed, conducted, in the absence of Rector Edward Washburn, by Dr. Rylance of St. Mark's Episcopal Church and Dr. Eigenbrodt of the General Theological Seminary. Members of the vestry, including Samuel B. Ruggles, joined the congregants in singing two of Niblo's favorite hymns, "I Would Not Live Alway" and "Rock of Ages," as their senior warden was mourned. The coffin was taken to Green-Wood, where the graveside attendees were few. Though a reporter for *The Sun* described the exterior and interior of the mausoleum in detail, the secret of the provenance of the "beautiful marble of a sleeping child" was kept, its presence unexplained.[153]

Niblo's will and a codicil thereto were promptly probated. He had outlived both of his brothers, John and Robert, as well as his wife. After providing $5,000 for permanent care of his mausoleum, he left low five-figure gifts to his brother John's two daughters and Reverend William D. Walker, pastor of Calvary Free Chapel. Low four-figure gifts and personal property were bequeathed to various other relatives, as well as to Mary and Charles Sylvester; Niblo's executors, Franklin Chandler and Jacob Lockman; and in support of Reverend Walker's work with poor congregants at the Free Chapel. Smaller gifts were made to several Calvary members.

The bulk of Niblo's estate, which totaled less than $300,000, went to the Young Men's Christian Association to support and expand its Niblo

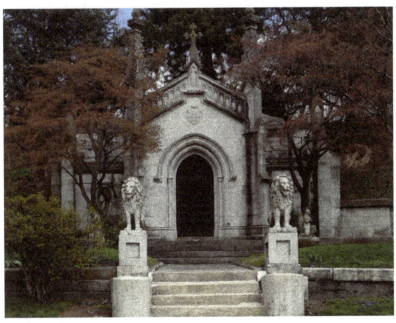

FIGURE 58: *The Niblo Mausoleum at Green-Wood Cemetery; Courtesy of Green-Wood Historic Fund.*

Library under the direction of Robert Hoe. Over the years, Hoe added countless fifteenth-century incunabula, sixteenth- and seventeenth-century bibles, and classical literature, but apparently the precious inventory was seldom used. Niblo's good intentions were honored for less than 30 years. On May 25 and 26, 1905, bids were taken in the East 20th Street auction rooms of the Merwin-Clayton Sales Company for the disposal of the Niblo Library. The YMCA decided to put the assets to better use and, perhaps concerned with public criticism, kept hidden the provenance of the collection.[154]

EPILOGUE

Niblo's name remained in common parlance for the seventeen years after his retirement from Niblo's Garden in 1861 until his death in 1878, chiefly through the marquee of that venue. Ultimately festooned with electric lights, it continued to form a bold presence on the Broadway façade of the Metropolitan Hotel, after being acquired by merchant A. T. Stewart and a succession of less well known businessmen. The hotel was sold to the Havemeyer family in 1895 and demolished for the construction of lofts and offices, and with that, only the memory of the thousands of performances in the storied temple of popular culture remained.

A burst of fame and even notoriety for the Niblo name had come in 1866, even though he was probably scandalized by the reasons. America's first so-called musical was brought to Niblo's Garden that year by theater operator William Wheatley, and ran for 474 performances. The show was based upon a book entitled *The Black Crook* by Charles Barras and set to music, much of it copied from existing tunes. Perhaps its most famous original number was "You Naughty, Naughty Men." A torrent of press accompanied the show's run at Niblo's, inevitably remarking upon the scantily clad (for the day) women on stage. Diarist George Templeton Strong remarked that

> Ballet, spectacle, machinery and pink legs are its chief constituents. The dialogue is senseless, the plot undiscoverable, and the music commonplace—plagiarism from the Grande Duchesse excepted . . . the dresses, properties, decorations and the like, are novel and lavish, except in the costumes of the ballet girls, which are the reverse of lavish in quantity, though various and pretty in design and color. A grand procession of fishes, oysters, and lobsters is very grotesque and carefully equipped. The final tableau or "transformation scene" is particularly elaborate and pretty. A scene shifter would call it gorgeous. In a meretricious sort of way it is quite artistic, with its slowly shifting masses of color, changing lights, and groups of good-looking young women (with very little on) nestling or hanging about everywhere. But the whole production depends for its success mainly on the well-formed lower extremities of female humanity. It is doubtless the

most showy, and the least draped specimen of what may be called the Feminine-Femoral School of Dramatic Art ever produced in New York. House packed—men mostly—and enthusiastic.[155]

It is doubtful that Niblo, then a warden and vestryman of Calvary Church in his late seventies, saw the show. Perhaps no one would have even recognized the modest, balding, bespectacled gentleman as he made his way down Broadway on one errand or another. One imagines Niblo turning his head in shame when mistaken congratulations were offered by ignorant well-wishers to a modest old man whose well-respected name was misused. Despite *The Black Crook*, Niblo's name remained a symbol of decent entertainment until the Havemeyer family tore Niblo's Garden to the ground.

NOTES

1. "Portraits of William Niblo," author unidentified, in *The Literary Collector* 2, no. 2 [presumably February 1901], 26–29.

2. Ibid.

3. William Niblo household, Seventh Census . . . 1850: New York, New York Co., New York City, Ward 14, National Archives Microfilm M432, roll 551, p. 26, #114-413.

4. Niblo's naturalization petition was filed in 1838, long after he sold the Bank Coffee House. The witness to the application, Philip Phoenix, a prominent New York merchant, swears that Niblo had resided in the United States since April 14, 1802, which would indicate that Niblo arrived in the country while at most twelve years old. See William Niblo petition for naturalization, 1838, New York County Court of Common Pleas, 17:164, dexigraph copy, National Archives and Records Administration—Northeast Branch, New York, New York. On the contrary, his 1878 death certificate attests to the fact that he had resided in the United States for 72 years. The death certificate attests to Ireland having been Niblo's birthplace, but my genealogical research is inconclusive, suggesting the existence of Scots ancestry also. See Certificate of Death 299154 issued by the New York City Department of Health on August 24, 1878.

5. See the *New-York Evening Post*, November 5, 1819.

6. The Bank Coffee House was located at the southwest corner of Pine and William Streets in the rear of the headquarters of the Bank of New York. After the end of the Revolutionary War, Tory sympathizer Frederick Philipse III was released from prison and reacquired title to his confiscated house. See I. N. Phelps Stokes, *The Iconography of Manhattan Island 1498–1909*, Vol. 5 (New York: Robert H. Dodd, 1926), 1566. See also William Alexander Duer, *New-York as it was, during the latter part of the last century* (Saint Nicholas Society of the City of New York, 1849), 9–10. See also deed from Edward P. and Sophia H. R. Terry of Hartford, Connecticut to Frederick Philips [*sic*] of Philipstown, New York, recorded on March 10, 1830, in Liber 258, Page 572, New York City Register's Office (hereafter NYCRO).

7. So listed in directories; also "Sloat Lane" in other ads and sources. King's establishment was named the Bell Tavern and was directly behind General Moreau's residence at 119 Pearl Street, corner of Slote Lane. The latter thoroughfare is now known as Beaver Street, running between William and Hanover Streets. See Joseph Alfred Scoville [pen name Walter Barrett, clerk], *The old merchants of New York City*, Vol. 1 (New York: Carleton, 1863), 337.

8. Numerous entries in the minutes of the Common Council for the years 1802–1811; see *Minutes of the Common Council of the City of New York 1784–1831*, Vol. 2, pp. 513, 548, 689; Vol. 3, pp. 12, 156, 297, 404, 450, 593, 639; Vol. 4, pp. 79, 105, 141, 236, 264, 314, 376, 468, 673; Vol. 5, pp. 223, 371, 505, 642; Vol. 6, pp. 92, 309, 429, 448, 449, 462, 581.

9. Mary Niblo appears in the extant surviving records of the First Presbyterian Church only in a ledger of graves whose contents were transferred from the Church's Forsyth Street burial ground in Manhattan to Cypress Hills Cemetery in Brooklyn in 1848. Her coffin was removed to Green-Wood Cemetery in 1854. Catherine King appears in the surviving records of the Church as early as August 31, 1809. These records contain no evidence of her husband David nor of their daughter Martha having been admitted as members of the congregation. William Niblo and Martha King's marriage is recorded in the ledger of marriages. The Church records I examined are housed in the Presbyterian Historical Society, Philadelphia.

10. The third structure was taken down and sold in pieces to a Jersey City church in 1844, and First Presbyterian moved to its current site at Fifth Avenue and 12th Street in Greenwich Village in that year.

11. See William H. Ukers, "History of Coffee in Old New York" in *All About Coffee* (New York: The Tea and Coffee Trade Journal Company), 1922, http://www.web-books.com/Classics/ON/B0/B701/18MB701.html.

12. New York City directories list a William Niblo as early as 1814–15 at 43, 45, and/or 47 Pine Street. These listings continue through 1828, with a separate Bank Coffee House listing beginning in 1819-20. Niblo worked for David King at King's "house of entertainment at the northwest corner of Nassau and Wall streets" across the street from the City Hall that preceded the 1814 structure still in use in City Hall Park. David King is listed along with the Bank Coffee House at 47 Pine Street only in 1820 and 1821. See "Reminiscences of the Old Bank Coffee House," an unidentified newspaper clipping appearing in Henry Onderdonk, Jr., *New York City in Olden Times, 1863* [scrapbook at The New York Public Library].

13. See Thomas Goodwin and Rufus Osgood Mason, *Sketches and Impressions, Musical Theatrical and Social, 1799–1885* (New York: G. P. Putnam's Sons, 1887), 277–78.

14. Ibid., 275 *et seq.*

15. The quoted material is taken from "Hotels in New York in 1828," transcribed in the W. Johnson Quinn Hotel Files at the New-York Historical Society, 1828 folder.

16. "The Ordinary" is an Anglicism used in contemporary journalism to mean a tavern that served regular meals.

17. Sir Joseph Banks, 1st Baronet, GCB, PRS (24 February [O.S. 13 February] 1743–19 June 1820), was an English naturalist, botanist and patron of the natural sciences. He took part in Captain James Cook's first great voyage (1768–1771). Banks is credited with the introduction to the Western world of eucalyptus, acacia, mimosa, and the genus named after him, Banksia. Approximately eighty species of plants bear Banks's name. Banks was also the leading founder of the African Association, a British organization dedicated to the exploration of Africa, and a member of the Society of Dilettanti, which helped to establish the Royal Academy. He also served as President of the Royal Society. Wikipe-

dia contributors, "Joseph Banks," *Wikipedia, The Free Encyclopedia*, http://en.wikipedia.org/wiki/Joseph_Banks (accessed April 6, 2014). Sir William Curtis, 1st Baronet (1752–1829), was a long-time member of Parliament, sheriff, alderman, and Lord Mayor of London. Wikipedia contributors, "William Curtis," *Wikipedia, The Free Encyclopedia*, http://en.wikipedia.org/wiki/Sir_William_Curtis,_1st_Baronet (accessed April 6, 2014).

18. Big Bone Lick is close to present-day Mammoth Cave, Kentucky.

19. "Lazaretto" probably refers to the area of Tinicum Township in Delaware County, Pennsylvania, where the first quarantine hospital of Philadelphia was established in 1799 after a more modest facility had stood there since 1743.

20. See Goodwin and Mason, *Sketches and Impressions*, 277–78.

21. How Ann Furey was allowed to sue Niblo in her own name for a civil claim in unclear. In general, under the English common law doctrine of *feme sole*, only unmarried women, be they widows, divorced, or never married, were empowered to sue in their own names in New York courts until late in the nineteenth century. Adult married women in mid-nineteenth-century America were still without most civil rights, and could only sue in civil court (even for divorce) when represented by a man (usually a relative) as their "next friend." (The death or divorce of a husband somehow suddenly rendered the wife sagacious and competent as she was before her marriage, qualifying her to represent herself in civil court, unassisted). Ms. Furey must have been unmarried at the time of the litigation.

22. See *Minutes of the Common Council of the City of New York*, Vol. 9, pp. 44, 682, 783; Vol. 11, p. 509; Vol. 12, pp. 292 , 713; Vol. 13, p. 497; Vol. 14, pp. 20, 97; Vol. 19, p. 407.

23. Michael and Ariane Batterberry, *On the Town in New York* (2nd ed.) (London: Routledge, 1999), 48.

24. Henry R. Stiles, *A History of the City of Brooklyn—Volume II*, published by subscription, Brooklyn, New York, 1869, 130–1 and map between 120–1.

25. The club moved up to the northern end of Manhattan by the end of the century.

26. Goodwin and Mason, *Sketches and Impressions*, 282–83. See also the *New-York Evening Post*, May 31, 1817; *The National Advocate*, June 26, 1815, July 24, 1815, April 22, 1817, and May 23, 1817; and the *Commercial Advertiser* (New York), May 27, 1814, and June 28, 1815.

27. See the *New-York Evening Post*, May 21, 1821; also Charles Haynes Haswell, *Memoirs of an octogenarian of the City of New York (1816–1860)* (New York: Harper and Brothers, 1896), 245.

28. Col. Thomas Picton, "Niblo's Garden," *New York Clipper*, April 25, 1868. Alderman Hall moved his training establishment to Harlem, and the site was occupied by a girl's equestrian school before Niblo acquired control.

29. See Thomas Allston Brown, *A History of the New York Stage*, Vol. 1 (New York: Dodd, Mead, 1903), 75. Stephen Van Rensselaer III (November 1, 1764–January 26, 1839) was

Lieutenant Governor of New York as well as a statesman and soldier, playing a major role as commander of federal forces in Quebec during the War of 1812, and famously defeated at the Battle of Queenston. He was also a landowner—the heir to one of the largest estates in the New York region—who took title to various parcels on the block in 1817 and 1826. His namesake son acquired additional parcels between 1840 and 1852 and sold ten of them to merchant prince A. T. Stewart in 1854.

30. Though one contemporary account asserts that the Columbian Gardens occupied Niblo's site, a perhaps more definitive scholarly account disputes this fact. According to Katy Matheson, Harmony Garden occupied the site in question in 1819, known two years later as Pavilion Gardens. See Katy Matheson, "Niblo's Garden and Its 'Concert Saloon,' 1828–1846," *Performing Arts Resources* 21 (1998): 61–62.

31. See Felix Barker and Peter Jackson, *The Pleasures of London* (London: London Topographical Society, 2008), 59–61.

32. Naomi Stubbs, *Cultivating National Identity Through Performance—American Pleasure Gardens and Entertainment* (New York: Palgrave Macmillan, 2013), 9.

33. John Flavel Mines, L.L.D., *A Tour Around New York and My Summer Acre, Being the Recreations of Mr. Felix Oldboy* (New York: Harper & Brothers, 1893), 133.

34. See *The National Advocate,* September 30, 1817, and August 3, 1819.

35. See Picton, "Niblo's Garden."

36. For a comprehensive discussion of the history of New York's pleasure gardens, see Thomas Myers Garrett, "A History of Pleasure Gardens in New York City 1700–1865," Ph.D. diss., New York University, 1978. As to unaccompanied women therein, see p. 608.

37. Goodwin and Mason, *Sketches and Impressions.*

38. Brown, *A History of the New York Stage*, 176. Brown mistakenly cites the year of the opening of the Sans Souci theater as 1827.

39. Matheson, "Niblo's Garden," 53. Public parks, other than the one immediately south of City Hall, were virtually nonexistent in New York in the early decades of the nineteenth century. Pleasure gardens, be they genteel or not, served as substitute public recreation spaces until Union and Tompkins Squares were created in 1833 and 1834, respectively. Bryant Park opened in 1846, and Central Park was developed only after 1857. The rise of public mass spectator sports in the latter half of the nineteenth century and the opening of public parks went hand-in-hand with the decrease in the number of pleasure gardens operating in New York.

40. Stubbs, *American Pleasure Gardens*, 53.

41. Matheson, "Niblo's Garden," 64, quoted from A. Gothamite, "Old Time Gardens," *New York Clipper*, n.d. (in Niblo's Garden file at the Museum of the City of New York).

42. *Albion* (New York), June 26, 1830, the *American* (New York), June 19, 1832, and the *New-York Evening Post*, June 12, 1830, as cited in Matheson, "Niblo's Garden," 63.

43. George C. D. Odell, *Annals of the New York Stage*, Vol. 3 (New York: Columbia University Press, 1928), 372–74.

44. Stubbs, *American Pleasure Gardens*, 69, 77–88. The term *bon ton* is cited by Stubbs from an article in the *New-York Spectator* of July 2, 1835.

45. Garrett, "A History of Pleasure Gardens," 615.

46. Stubbs, *American Pleasure Gardens*, 70–71, 77.

47. George Foster, *New York by Gas-Light and Other Urban Sketches*, ed. Stuart Blumin (Berkeley: University of California Press, 1990), 156–57. First published 1850.

48. Goodwin and Mason, *Sketches and Impressions*, 283–84.

49. Garrett, "A History of Pleasure Gardens," i–iv.

50. Col. Thomas Picton, "Niblo's and Its Surroundings," *New York Clipper*, May 9, 1868.

51. Stubbs, *American Pleasure Gardens*, 10.

52. Garrett, "A History of Pleasure Gardens," 7.

53. Edwin G. Burrows and Mike Wallace, *Gotham: A History of New York City to 1898* (London: Oxford University Press, 1999), 585–86.

54. See Tom D. Crouch, *The Eagle Aloft: Two Centuries of the Balloon in America* (Washington, DC: Smithsonian Institution Press, 1983), 144. Garrett, "A History of Pleasure Gardens," 610, cites the incident as occurring the day before and refers to an article in the *New-York American* of July 22, 1828.

55. *Hannah Johnson vs. William Niblo*, Index No. 1829/545.

56. The incident is mentioned in Garrett, "A History of Pleasure Gardens," 610, cited from the *Commercial Advertiser* (New York), September 9, 1841.

57. See Goodwin and Mason, *Sketches and Impressions*, 282. See Figure 17, page 35.

58. See conveyance from Ramsay Crooks to William Niblo in conveyance Liber 291, Pages 77–87, NYCRO.

59. *Minutes of the Common Council of the City of New York*, Vol. 9, p. 77. A rudimentary system of water mains existed in what is now Lower Manhattan before the construction of the dam at Croton Falls, New York, and the aqueduct that brought fresh water to the city in 1842. Fire protection was vastly improved with a much greater supply of water and the installation of a network of mains and laterals that forms the foundations of the modern-day New York water supply.

60. Daguerre, better known for his later inventions in photography, created yet another improvement, presented in London in 1823. The Diorama was a revolving auditorium in which a 72-foot-wide painting was shown at the end of a 45-foot-long tunnel. Translucent canvas and back lighting created impressive effects as the scenes changed with the rotation of the seating platform. Yet another variation, invented in New York and brought to London a few years later, was the Cosmorama, the London version of which consisted

of a salon fitted with eight small windows with convex lenses, allowing viewers to see enlarged views of storms at sea, great waterfalls, and monuments of antiquity in apparent life size. See Barker and Jackson, *The Pleasures of London*, 110–13.

61. Picton, "Niblo's and Its Surroundings." For details of other dioramas and the like in New York in that decade, see George C. D. Odell, *Annals of the New York Stage*, Vol. 4 (New York: Columbia University Press, 1928), 43.

62. A. H. Saxon, *P. T. Barnum, The Legend and the Man* (New York: Columbia University Press, 1989), 91. Blackface minstrel shows also became popular in London by the mid-1840s. See also Barker and Jackson, *The Pleasures of London*, 134–35.

63. Phineas Taylor Barnum, *The Autobiography of P. T. Barnum, Clerk, Merchant, Editor, Showman* (London: Ward & Lock, 1855), 54 *et seq.*

64. Freeman's death was the subject of an inquisition by the coroner of New York County, whose twelve impaneled jurors rendered a verdict of accidental death on the same day. See *New York County Coroner Inquests,* microfilm roll 9, September 1835–July 1836, at the New York City Municipal Archives.

65. *New-York Evening Post,* September 18, 1835, and *Long Island* [New York] *Farmer,* September 23, 1835.

66. Banvard's panorama of the Mississippi River was advertised as being depicted on three miles of canvas and shown in the Panorama Building during July 1847. See Odell, *Annals of the New York Stage*, Vol. 4, p. 389.

67. Picton, "Niblo's Garden."

68. See http://content.winterthur.org:2011/cdm/compoundobject/collection/watsonfam/id/826/rec/1 for a digital copy of the Watson diary, at page 9 therein.

69. Picton, "Niblo's Garden."

70. The Pulaski Cadets, http://www.pulaskicadets.org/history.html.

71. Matheson, "Niblo's Garden," 79–80. N.B.: Matheson's statement that the annual gathering was held at the Bank Coffee House from 1818 to 1831 may be in error. Niblo disposed of his interest in it in 1828.

72. Picton, "Niblo's and Its Surroundings."

73. Ibid.

74. Col. Thomas Picton, "Niblo's and the Dancing Days of Yore," *New York Clipper,* May 2, 1868.

75. The American Institute Fair was held from 1829 until 1897 and was considered the first world's fair. It moved from Niblo's Garden to New York's Crystal Palace in 1854. Wikipedia contributors, "American Institute Fair," *Wikipedia, The Free Encyclopedia,* http://en.wikipedia.org/wiki/American_Institute_Fair, accessed April 21, 2014, citing F. W. Wile, ed., *A Century of Industrial Progress* (New York: American Institute of the City

of New York), 1928; see also Museum of the City of New York, http://mcnyblog.org/tag/american-institute-fair/, accessed April 21, 2014.

76. Picton, "Niblo's and Its Surroundings."

77. See conveyance dated January_, 1841, recorded in NYCRO on January 12, 1841, in Liber 411, Page 302, and also Odell, *Annals of the New York Stage,* Vol. 4, p. 47. As to attachment of income, see *Stodart and Bacon vs. Niblo,* New York County Chancery Court Index #BM 1284-D, docketed November 4, 1836.

78. The term was employed in France to describe short dramatic presentations that became popular there in the early decades of the nineteenth century. The American usage of the term for an assortment of acts interspersed with light musical offerings came into common parlance much later in the century.

79. Odell, *Annals of the New York Stage,* Vol. 4, p. 181.

80. Picton, "Niblo's and the Dancing Days."

81. Though the financial arrangements between Niblo and various performance promoters are unclear in most broadsides advertising shows at the Garden in the 1830s, litigation records make clear in certain instances that Niblo occasionally acted only as landlord. See, e.g., *William Niblo vs. Vincent Schmidt,* New York County Clerk Judgment Index No. 1835: N-17, ditto: New York City Court of Common Pleas 1833 #854 and 1834 #1086.

82. Odell, *Annals of the New York Stage,* Vol. 4, pp. 265, 431. An essay entitled *19th Century American Theater,* available online in the Digital Collections of the University of Washington at http://content.lib.washington.edu/19thcenturyactorsweb/essay.html#top, provides a comprehensive overview of the provenance, styles, and development of theatrical styles and venues in the United States during the early as well as mid-century decades. A benefit stage for a theater owner was uncommon unless he or she was also a thespian.

83. Editorial quoted from issue of July 19, 1834, in Cynthia A. Hoover, "A Trumpet Battle at Niblo's Pleasure Garden," *The Musical Quarterly* 55, no. 3 (July 1969): 384–95.

84. Odell, *Annals of the New York Stage,* Vol. 4, pp. 330, 428, 595.

85. Brown, *A History of the New York Stage,* 179.

86. Odell, *Annals of the New York Stage,* Vol. 4, pp. 64–65.

87. *New-York Daily Tribune,* September 18, 1846.

88. *New-York Daily Tribune,* September 19, 1846.

89. Ibid.

90. Picton, "Niblo's Garden."

91. Odell, *Annals of the New York Stage,* Vol. 4, p. 243.

92. The entry for September 18, 1846, in the manuscript version of Philip Hone's diary is cited in Matheson, "Niblo's Garden," 68, as providing an account of the fire that ends on a disturbing note: "Destruction of Niblo's—This delightful place of public resort was

totally destroyed by fire this morning at 1/2 past four o'clock. The Theatre in which the Ravels were bringing crowded houses every night; the spacious Saloon . . . The fine collection of plants indigenous and exotic and all the productions of poor Niblo's taste and assiduity in administering to the gratification of the people of New York, all were swept away in a couple of hours and are now lying, with the two large houses he occupied and the adjoining shops, a black and smoking plain of undistinguishable destruction. The brick building on the north west corner of the ground was burnt down and the splendid Racket Court Club House was saved only by great exertions. Niblo's lease is, I understand, nearly expired. He cannot afford to renew it worse [?] rebuild upon it, for a large Hotel, an Opera House, or a Cathedral . . . I have a fact in relation to the origin of this fire, which I shall write down and preserve among my papers in case it may be wanted hereafter I have reason to believe it was not accidental."

93. *New-York Daily Tribune,* September 22, 1846.

94. *New-York Daily Tribune,* November 23, 1847, and December 1, 1847.

95. *New-York Daily Tribune,* July 22, 1848.

96. *Account of the Terrible and Fatal Riot at the New-York Astor Place Opera House On the night of May 10, 1849* (New York: H. M. Ranney, 1849); see also Richard Moody, *The Astor Place Riot* (Bloomington: Indiana University Press, 1958), 101–4, 133–36.

97. Nigel Cliff's *The Shakespeare Riots* (New York: Random House, 2007) provides a comprehensive account of the socio-cultural framework of the Astor Place riot. Hackett's relationship with Forrest is noted on p. 177.

98. Ibid., 209–15.

99. Ibid.

100. News of the riot was an international sensation and was covered extensively in the local and distant press. This statistic is taken from reporting in *The New York Herald,* May 12, 1849.

101. Ibid.

102.   In the strength of your might, from each mountain and valley,
       Sons of Freedom, arise! the time is at hand—
       Around Liberty's standard, we'll rally, we'll rally;
       The Star-Spangled Banner floats over the land.

       Then let the proud Eagle spread his wings wide asunder,
       And burst from the tramels which strive to enchain
       If we rise in our strength, if we speak but in thunder
       The bit of strip'd bunting will flourish again.

       For our Rights and our Laws, we'll stand firm and united;
       The blood of our Father's shall ne'er be forgot—

> The Faith and the Honor they sacredly plighted,
> Shall never be tarnished by Anarchy's blot;
>
> Around Liberty's standard, we'll rally, we'll rally;—
> Old Tippecanoe, boys, the watch word shall be;
> Its echo will thunder from each mountain and valley
> Of the Home of the brave—the Land of the free.
>
> —"Grand National Whig Song" (author unknown) in *The Harrison and Log Cabin Song Book* (Columbus, OH: I. N. Whiting, 1840).

In the *New-York American* (March 19, 1840), H. Russell announced the indefinite postponement of his concert scheduled for that evening at Niblo's Saloon because of the proprietor's sudden late and peremptory refusal to allow the "Grand National Whig Song" to be performed. At a subsequent event that year, opponents of Whig Party presidential candidate William Henry Harrison fomented a riot outside Niblo's Garden when a Whig parade approached the premises. The violence was celebrated by diarist and Whig supporter George Templeton Strong in his diary entry of May 11, 1840. See *The Diary of George Templeton Strong*, Vol. 1, ed. Allan Nevins and Milton Halsey Thomas (New York: Macmillan, 1952), 137–38.

103. John Purdy Blair, Jr., "Productions at Niblo's Garden Theater 1849–1862 (New York City)," Ph.D. diss., University of Georgia, 1982, 6–9, 22.

104. *New-York Daily Tribune*, December 4, 1850, December 28, 1850, and January 1, 1851. See also Blair, "Productions at Niblo's Garden," 48.

105. *The Scientific American* (New York) 7 (issue 52), September 11, 1852.

106. Ellen W. Kramer, "Contemporary Descriptions of New York City and Its Public Architecture ca. 1850," *Journal of the Society of Architectural Historians* 27, no. 4 (December 1968): 274. The advertisement for a June 1, 1852, opening is included in the 1852 book *Views in America, Great Britain, Switzerland, Turkey, Italy, the Holy Land, Etc.* (New York: J. Milton Emerson, 1852), and probably represents the hopes, later not met, of an early June opening.

107. Blair, "Productions at Niblo's Garden," 219.

108. Ibid., 106.

109. Ibid., 238–48. See also Brown, *A History of the New York Stage*, 180–1.

110. Thomas Dickinson, "Billy Niblo and His Famous Garden," *The Theatre Magazine* 7 (1907): 214. Patti was, according to other sources, eight years old by the time of her New York debut. Her recollection of the performance, shaving a year off her age, was transcribed in the magazine article more than half a century later.

111. Timothy J. Gilfoyle, *City of Eros—New York City, Prostitution, and the Commercialization of Sex, 1790–1920* (New York: W. W. Norton, 1992), 120–1.

112. Paul Preston, "Palmo's Opera House," *New York Clipper,* August 15, 1868.

113. Blair, "Productions at Niblo's Garden," 93.

114. Ibid., 164–66.

115. *New-York Times,* May 5, 1854.

116. Brown, *A History of the New York Stage,* 183.

117. Ibid., 189.

118. Ibid., 259–74.

119. See *The Scientific American* (New York) 3 (n.s., issue 2), July 7, 1860.

120. *New-York Times,* June 26, 1860.

121. Brown, *A History of the New York Stage,* 191. See also George C. D. Odell, *Annals of the New York Stage,* Vol. 7 (New York: Columbia University Press, 1931), 396.

122. See the *New-York Evening Post,* January 19, 1825. Mary Niblo's remains were reinterred at Brooklyn's Cemetery of Evergreens in 1848, and removed to the Niblo mausoleum at Green-Wood in 1854. See *Record of remains removed from the burial ground in Forsyth Street belonging to the First Presbyterian Church to Cypress Hills Cemetery Long Island. Also to private plots and the church vaults on 5th Avenue,* Collections of the Presbyterian Historical Society, Philadelphia.

123. See *The First Annual Report of the Board of Managers of The American Bible Society, Presented May 8, 1817* (New York: Printed for the Society by J. Seymour, 1817), 34; *First Annual Report of the Society for the Encouragement of Faithful Domestic Servants* (New York: Printed by D. Fanshaw at the American Tract Society's House, 1826), 28–31; *Second Annual Report of the Society for the Encouragement of Faithful Domestic Servants* (New York: Printed by D. Fanshaw at the American Tract Society's House, 1827), 2–7, 10, 29–32. N.B.: The *Second Annual Report,* which indicates its publication in 1827, makes reference to events in 1828.

124. Davis was manumitted on October 20, 1817. See *The New York Genealogical and Biographical Record* 109, no. 3 (July 1978), 149.

125. Samuel M. Shoemaker, *Calvary Church, Yesterday and Today—A Centennial History* (London: Fleming H. Revell Company, 1936), 3. Unless otherwise cited to different sources, much of the factual information in this chapter is taken from Shoemaker's comprehensive work. I have also minutely inspected the extant handwritten records of Calvary Church at the Parish House.

126. Several accounts of his demeanor and importance appear in the diaries of Philip Hone and George Templeton Strong (both students of McVickar's at Columbia).

127. Renwick went on to design St. Patrick's Cathedral at 49th Street and Fifth Avenue, the original structures of the Smithsonian Museum, the Corcoran Art Gallery in Washington, D.C., New York's St. Bartholomew's Church, and several buildings at Vassar College.

128. The document is among the papers of Francis Lister Hawks held at the New-York Historical Society, Box 1, Folder 3.

129. Shoemaker, *Calvary Church,* 94.

130. Ibid., 99.

131. Niblo purchased two lots in this location in 1859. See Hugh Maxwell to William Niblo, conveyance Liber 779, Page 252; also deed to Niblo from 1844 in conveyance Liber 442, Page 583, NYCRO. Which if any of these parcels were acquired for or donated to Calvary for the 23rd Street Chapel is unclear. Niblo's will is dated June 7, 1875, and was admitted to probate in New York County Surrogate's Court in August 1878.

132. Haswell, *Memoirs of an octogenarian,* 476.

133. The quoted material is taken from an entry of January 19, 1861, transcribed in Shoemaker, *Calvary Church,* 101-3.

134. For a thorough account of Montez's last days, see Ishabel Ross, *The Uncrowned Queen—Life of Lola Montez* (New York: Harper and Row, 1972). The circumstances of Montez's illness and death as well as her living accommodations and friendly relationship with Maria Buchanan are substantially disputed in *Lola Montes—The Tragic Story of a Liberated Woman,* comp. M. Cannon (Melbourne, Australia: Heritage Publications, 1973). This volume asserts that Buchanan took merciless advantage of Montez in the latter's final months, moving her to one sorry lodging after another and fleecing the dying woman of her earthly possessions.

135. Benson J. Lossing, *History of New York City* (New York: The Perine Engraving and Publishing Co., 1884). Lossing claims that Hawks returned to be Rector of the Chapel of the Holy Saviour in 1865, but this account is perhaps at variance with Shoemaker's work, which states that the cornerstone of that Chapel was laid by Reverend Hawks on September 4, 1866.

136. See Evert A. Duyckinck, *A Memorial of Francis L. Hawks, D.D., LL.D.,* New-York Historical Society, New York, 1871.

137. *Trow's New York City Directory 1855-56* lists John Niblo as a liquor merchant in business at Crosby and Houston Streets, adjacent to Niblo's Garden.

138. For 1822 statistics, see Henry Wysham Lanier, *A Century of Banking in New York 1822-1922* (New York: The Gilliss Press, 1922), 24; for 1850, see William A. Darling, *List of Persons, Copartnerships, and Corporations Who were Taxed on Seventeen Thousand Five Hundred Dollars and Upwards in the City of New York, in the Year 1850* (New York: John F. Whitney, 1850), 65.

139. See BM 390-F 1833 New York City Chancery Court: *John Fisher and Richard Fisher vs. William Niblo,* filed August 26, 1833. The Fishers had obtained a judgment against Niblo for $166.60 for goods manufactured and sold to Niblo. The sheriff tried to levy against various apparent assets of Niblo but was unable to find any, and claimed that

Niblo willingly frustrated execution. An injunction was requested to force Niblo to be examined in court to disclose his assets and prevent other creditors from gaining prior advantage. Niblo was said by the plaintiff to live in style and to own Niblo's Hotel and Niblo's Garden. In BM 1284-D 1836 New York City Chancery Court, *William Dubois, William Stodart and George Bacon vs William Niblo*, the plaintiffs had obtained judgment against Niblo for $98.36 for nonperformance of certain unspecified promises and undertakings. Once again, the sheriff could not find assets upon which to levy. Niblo was said to have control of a large quantity of personal property supposedly assigned for the benefit of other creditors, as well as funds coming in from rental of Niblo's Garden to the American Institute Fair that exceeded the amount of the judgment. An order of examination was granted against Niblo.

140. It is unclear when Crooks acquired the rights to the personal property and realty that he conveyed to Niblo in 1832. It is a matter of public record that Niblo opened Niblo's Garden on its site in 1828. Perhaps he and Crooks had an arrangement prior to that evidenced by the instruments recorded in 1832. See conveyance dated and recorded November 15, 1832, in Liber 290, Page 111, and that dated and recorded November 17, 1832, in Liber 291, Page 77, NYCRO. The second instrument details a lease of the two buildings and a back house then standing at 576 Broadway, plus the lots upon which they sit, and 18 other nearby lots at a total rent of $2,800 per year, for a term of 18 months. For the litigation, see *Ramsay Crooks vs. William Niblo*, New York Supreme Court N-26 1832.

141. *William Niblo vs. Thomas M. Walmsley*, BM 172-W New York County Chancery Court pleading dated September 22, 1846

142. Alexis de Tocqueville, *Letters from America*, http://hudsonreview.com/2013/03/letters-from-america/#.UnozB5wo7IV.

143. See conveyances, all NYCRO conveyance books: Liber 455, Page 30; Liber 452, Page 388; Liber 62, Page 617; Liber 480, Page 81; Liber 610, Page 369; Liber 625, Page 460; Liber 852, Page 453; Liber 35, Page 342; Liber 764, Page 436; Liber 866, Page 327; Liber 699, Page 83; Liber 814, Pages 293 and 323; Liber 616, Page 484.

144. It is unclear from the conveyancing instrument whether or not Niblo conveyed the lot to the National Academy as a charitable act. See deed recorded November 21, 1861 in conveyance Liber 841, Page 591.

145. The façade stands there today along with another architectural relic integrated therein: the marble balustrades from the Fifth Avenue and 34th Street mansion of merchant A.T. Stewart, who was proprietor of Niblo's Garden for several decades after Niblo's retirement.

146. See *Rode's New York City Directory 1852–53*. Other purchases were miscellaneous lots between 18th and 19th Streets west of Fifth Avenue, and a large parcel on the south side of 31st Street between Third and Lexington Avenues.

147. Katy Matheson asserts that Martha and William probably had at least one child, who

did not survive them, but acknowledges that none are mentioned as survivors in the obituaries of heirs in the relevant documents. See Matheson, "Niblo's Garden," 55-56.

148. See *The First Annual Report of the Board of Managers of the American Bible Society, Presented May 8, 1817* (New York: Printed for the Society by J. Seymour, 1817), 34; *Biographical Sketches of Hezekiah Jarvis, Noah Jarvis, George A. Jarvis and William Jarvis From The Encyclopaedia of Contemporary Biography of New York*, Vol. 5 (New York: Atlantic Publishing and Engraving Company, 1887), 5 and plate.

149. The Almshouse was situated in City Hall Park until 1816. I am indebted to Julie Miller, author of *Abandoned: Foundlings in Nineteenth Century America* (New York: New York University Press, 2008), for all of the information concerning the Almshouse itself and its practices, as well as for pointing the way to the original ledgers of the institution stored at New York City's Municipal Archives, where I recapitulated Miller's primary source research concerning Sarah Jane Hannan and William Niblo, *père et fils*.

150. See instrument recorded in conveyance Liber 1466, Page 61, NYCRO.

151. The probated will and codicil are contained in the records of the New York County Surrogate's Court in Liber 256, Page 442.

152. This account is taken from Goodwin and Mason, *Sketches and Impressions*, 290-1.

153. *The Sun* (New York), August 25, 1878.

154. *New-York Times*, May 7, 1905. See also *American Book Prices—Current*, Vol. 11, *Compiled From the Auctioneers' Catalogues by Luther S. Livingston* (New York: Dodd, Mead & Company, 1905), xvii.

155. *The Diary of George Templeton Strong*, Vol. 4, p. 183, entry of January 29, 1868. For a fuller account of the production of *The Black Crook* and the resultant public controversy, see Cecil Smith, *Musical Comedy in America: From The Black Crook to South Pacific* (New York: Methuen, 1950), 7-13.

ACKNOWLEDGMENTS

This volume is my third sizable undertaking since 2000 in writing New York City history, and as with the two previous ventures, my wife, Frances Stern, has been my constant and reliable companion, critic, and editor, in the overall conception, planning, research, and writing of the work. Without her lucid intelligence, critical eye, and loyal partnership, none of these works could have been brought to fruition.

Green-Wood Cemetery Resident Historian Jeffrey Richman has also been my intellectual partner and companion in each of the three books. Jeff introduced me to William Niblo many years ago and has supported and encouraged this work without fail. My other colleagues and supporters at Green-Wood are due a public expression of gratitude once again: President Richard Moylan, Corporate Secretary Jane Cuccurullo, Director of Development and Marketing Lisa Alpert, Director of Buildings and Grounds Arthur Presson, Manager of Programs and Membership Chelsea Dowell, and Archivist and Genealogist Theresa LaBianca have all been indispensable parts of this multiyear enterprise, which encompasses not only this volume but also multiple public re-creations of Niblo's Garden on the grounds of the Cemetery. Michael Burke, long-time friend of Green-Wood, played an invaluable early role in encouraging this project and valuing its premise and promise, as did Green-Wood aficionados and my performance partners Alyson Pou, Suzanne Wray, and Nadine Stewart.

Research is a tremendously rewarding, often frustrating task in writing nineteenth-century New York City history, and many individuals as well as the staffs of several institutions deserve credit for their tireless and invaluable contributions. First and foremost is my genealogist friend par excellence, Roger Joslyn, CG, FASB. Roger's delight in carrying out a very difficult assignment sent me on my way with a smile. Kenneth Cobb and staff of the New York City Municipal Archives were dependable and vital in the early process, as were Joseph Van Nostrand and Bruce Abrams of the New York County Clerk's Division of Old Records. Joseph Ditta and his colleagues at the New-York Historical

Society Library have been an overwhelming aid to this work, as have been Sarah Henry, Autumn Nyiri, and Morgen Stevens-Garmon of the Museum of the City of New York, and the staff of the Presbyterian Historical Society in Philadelphia. Wayne Kempton, historian of the New York Episcopal Archdiocese, is due my thanks, and Reverend Jacob Smith, Anna Mosby Coleman, and Marcia Behrmann of Manhattan's Calvary Episcopal Church helped me immeasurably in establishing the history of Niblo's participation in that distinguished body of worship. Connie King and Linda August at the Library Company of Philadelphia provided prompt, thorough, and courteous input and assistance with their wonderful collections of theater broadsides and libretti that shed light on Niblo's multitudinous productions.

In the midst of the first draft of this work, I stumbled upon Julie Miller's *Abandoned: Foundlings in Nineteenth-Century New York City*, published in 2008. Miller's assiduous scholarship in the New York City Municipal Archives turned up evidence of a sorry chapter in William Niblo's life that forms one of the most fascinating parts of this volume.

The Victorian Society of American (Metro NYC Chapter) and the Irish American History Association have both taken a healthy interest in this project, and for that I am grateful.

As this work entered its final stages, I became aware, through Don B. Wilmeth, editor of Palgrave Macmillan's Palgrave Studies in Theater History and Performance, of its very recently published history of pleasure gardens in America. Professor Naomi J. Stubbs (of LaGuardia Community College of the City University of New York) and her *Cultivating National Identity Through Performance—American Pleasure Gardens and Entertainment* were wonderful to encounter and most helpful in tying together important underlying cultural forces so central to William Niblo's life and career.

My closest reader and valued colleague, Professor Patricia Cline Cohen, chair emeritus of the UCSB History Department, supported this project, as she has my previous two books, with unflagging energy and perspicacity. I am indebted to Pat beyond measure for her 14-year-long encouragement and respect for my undertakings. I walk in her footsteps with pleasure.

In producing this volume, two individuals have been of great assistance: my long-time designer and compositor Jerry Kelly has produced a third magnificent volume, abreast of all the technological changes that have washed over the publishing world since I first started working with him in late 2006. Editor Janice Fisher is a new acquaintance, and a brilliant one at that. I am grateful for her attentions.

On a deeper level, three individuals deserve a public expression of my unbounded gratitude. My parents, Rose Polonsky Feldman and the late Cyrus Feldman, loved and supported my intellectual endeavors unconditionally since my earliest years. Their excitement at my accomplishments, be they in the business or academic worlds, with history, law, and languages, continues to fuel my fire.

Lastly, I wish to acknowledge my final employer in the business world, Stephen L. Green, founder of the SLGreen Realty Trust, for whom I worked for 13 years, helping build an inconsequential little commercial property owner in Manhattan into the city's largest owner of office buildings in 2014. Steve supported me and taught me many things along that arduous path, not the least of which was how to seize an opportunity and sell it, to myself and others. For that I am especially grateful.

INDEX

Academy of Music 65
Albert, Prince 47
Albion 47
Alboni, Marietta 69
Alhamra [sic] Hall 53
American Bible Society 72, 87, 92
American Eclipse (horse) 22
American Institute Fair 45 fig., 46, 53
Arion Society 70 fig.
Astor, John Jacob 28, 30, 32, 38, 76
Astor, Mrs. John Jacob 77
Astor Place Opera House and Riot 53–60
Atlantic Garden 16
Bank Coffee House 9, 15–18, 21–22, 24, 25, 43, 72, 83, 84, 86,
Bank of New York (figure) 14 fig., 99 n6
Banks, Sir Joseph 18
Banvard panorama 104 n66
Barras, Charles 97
Barker, Robert 38
Barnum, P. T. 38–40, 78
Bassford, Abraham 90
Bayard Farm 27
"Bedouin Arabs" 51, 52
Beekman, William 77
Beers, Joseph 76
Bell Tavern 44, 99 n7
"Belshazzar's Feast" 38
Bennett, James Godron 57
Bermondsey Spa 28
Betrand, Robert 52
Black, Bill 24
Black Crook 97–98
Blackwell's Island 92
Blitz, Signor Antonio 12
Blondin, Charles 50, 64
Bloomingdale 73
Board of the Domestic and Foreign Missionary Society 74

Bollingbrook Hotel 83
"Bombardment of Antwerp" 34
Bowery B'hoys 50, 54, 56, 71
Bowery Theater 55, 56
Bowling Green Garden 28
Booth, Edwin 48, 64, 70
Bristow, George F. 67
Broadway Theatre 56
Bryant's Minstrels 64
Buchanan, Maria 79, 80, 80 fig.
Burford, Robert 38
Burton, William 46 fig., 48, 64, 65
Calvary Episcopal Church 12, 72–81, 81 fig., 86, 87, 90, 94, 98
Calvary Free Chapel 95
Campagnologian Bell Ringers 50
Capelli, Signor 40
Carl Schurz Park 86
Castle Garden 34, 41
Catherwood, Frederick 38
Cemetery of Evergreens 108 n122
Chandler, Franklin 95
Chapel of the Holy Saviour 80
Chippendale, William 56
Christy's Minstrels 53
Church of the Mediator 77
City Guard 53
City (Hall) Park 16, 38, 59, 111 n149
City Hotel 44, 83
Cline, Herr Andre 31, 50, 67
Clinton, DeWitt 31
Coliseum 38
Colombian Gardens 27, 29
Colonial Dames of America 25
Columbia College of Physicians and Surgeons 78
Congress Hall Hotel 36, 83
Contoit's New York Garden 34
Contoit's Stables 90

115

Cooper, James Fenimore 30, 33
Cooper, James G. 10 fig., 11
Cooper, Peter 73, 75
Corbyn, Wardle 48
Cosmorama 104 n60
Crescent Water 12, 91
Crooks, Ramsay 36, 72, 84–85, 85 fig.
Croton Receiving Reservoir 75
Croton Water Commission 38
Crystal Palace 104 n75
Curtis, Sir William 18
Cushman, Charlotte 48, 64, 70
Cypress Hills Cemetery 100 n9
Daguerre, Louis 103 n60
Davis, Henry 73
Delacroix, Joseph 28, 32, 34
Delafield, John 32
Delafield, Mrs. Richard 77
De Loutherbourg, Philippe 38
"Departure of the Israelites from Egypt" 37, 37 fig.
De Peyster, Estelle 87
De Peyster, Frederic 73
Diorama 103 n60
Dixon, George Washington 76
Dodworth, Harvey 67
Dupont, Thomas 73–74
Durand, Asher 88
Earle, David 25
Eidophusikon 38
Emmet, Thomas Addis 75
Exchange (coffee house) 16
Fellows Opera House 64
First Presbyterian Church 15, 72, 100 n9, n10
Flood, Michael 21
Forrest, Edwin 48, 53 fig., 55–56, 70–71
Fossett, James 25
Foster, George 33
Freeman, Isaac 40
Furey, Ann 21

Gambati, Alessandro 42, 50
General Theological Seminary 73
Gibbes, Charlotte Augusta 76
Gilbert, Eliza (Lola Montez) 79
Gilfert, Charles 31
Goelet, Peter 88, 88 fig.
Goodwin, Thomas 33
Grace Church 75
Gracie, Archibald Jr. 74
Gracie, Archibald Sr. 74
Gracie, Robert 74, 77
"Grand National Whig Song" 59
Great Fire of 1835 15
Greatorex, Henry Wellington 78
Green-Wood Cemetery 9, 11, 80, 84, 91, 93 fig., 94 fig., 95, 95 fig., 100 n9, 108 n122
Hackett, James H. 53, 56, 106 n97
Hall, Charles Henry 27
Hamblin, Thomas 56
Handel's Messiah 32
Hampstead Wells 28
Hannan, Sarah Jane 92, 94
Harmony Garden 102 n30
Harrison, Benjamin Johns 45 fig.
Harrison, William Henry 107 n102
Havemeyer family 97, 98
Hawks, Rev. Francis Lister 76–81, 78 fig., 81 fig.
Heron, Matilda 64
Heth, Joice 39–40
Hoboken Turtle Club 23
Hoe, Robert 95
Hoffman, Ogden 75
Hollyer, Samuel 17 fig., 20 fig.
Hone, Philip 32, 105 n92, 108 n126
Hundred Pound Note, The 31
Hutchins, John 16
Il Antonio Diavolo 42
Irving, Henry 48
Jackson, Andrew 22, 31

Japanese delegation 68 fig., 71
Jarvis, Noah 92
Javelli, Leon 50
Jefferson, Joseph 48, 57
Jefferson Market Courthouse 42
Johnson, Madame Hannah 31, 35
Kean, Charles 48
Kean, Edmund 50
Kearny brothers 75
Kearny, Philip 74
Keene's Theater 47 fig., 64
Kemble, Charles 48, 55
Kensington House 24, 24 fig.
King, Catherine 11, 15, 91
King, Charles (singer) 32
King, Charles (Columbia University) 75
King, David 15, 16, 18, 92
King, Martha (Niblo) 11, 12, 13, 15, 87, 91, 92, 93
King's Arms 16
Leonard, Allen 46
Le Gascon a Trois Visages 52
Lehman, Adelaide (aka Adeline and Adele) 54, 63
Leland brothers 64
"Les Vaudevilles" 47
Lind, Jenny 78
Lindsay, R. W. 39
Lockman, Jacob 95
Lucia di Lammermoor 50
Lyman, Levi 39
Macbeth 56-57
Macready, William 53 fig., 55-57, 59, 70
McVickar, John 73, 108 n126
Madame Otto 41, 42
Magic Trumpet (or The Invisible Harlequin), The 62
Marble Hall 64
Marine Baths 23, 24 fig.
Martin, John 38
Marylebone Gardens 28

Mason, R. Osgood 33
Max Maretzek's Italian Opera Company 64
Maxwell, Hugh 109 n131
Mazzeppa 65
Merchants (coffee house) 16
Merritt, Willis 23
Merwin-Clayton Sales Company 96
Metropolitan Hotel 61, 61figs., 62 figs., 63, 67, 68, 71, 83, 97
"Military Grounds" 42
Milliners (or The Hungarian Rendezvous), The 62
Montez, Lola 79, 79 fig., 60
Montgomery Hall 42
Morse, Samuel F. B. 88
Mount Vernon Hotel 24, 25 figs.
National Academy of Design 88, 89 fig.
National Hotel 83
National Theater 26
New York City Almshouse 48
New York Female Tract Society 72
New York Light Guard 42
Niblo, Eliza 93
Niblo, John (father) 15
Niblo, John (brother) 15, 95
Niblo Library (YMCA) 95-96
Niblo, Martha King 11, 12, 13, 15, 87, 91, 108 n122
Niblo, Mary 15, 72, 91
Niblo, Robert 15, 95
Niblo, William Henry (son) 92-93
Nixon's Circus 66 fig.
Norma 50
Norton, John Thompson 27
Onderdonk, Henry Jr. 17, 20
Our Lady of Lourdes 88, 89 fig.
Palmo's Opera House 65
Panorama Building 40
Park Theater 16, 17
Patti, Adelina 64
Pavilion Gardens 102 n30

Philipse, Frederick 14 fig., 15, 21
Phoenix, Philip 99 n4
Picton, Col. Thomas 29, 40, 45
"Polkamania" 51
Pulaski Cadets 42
Pyne-Harrison Opera 64
Pyne, Louisa 67
Ranelagh Gardens 14, 28
Ravel family 42, 47, 50, 52, 62, 63, 64, 67
Renwick, James Jr., 75
Rip Van Winkle (opera) 67
Roberts, David 37, 38, 40
Roosevelt, Cornelius 88
Ruggles, Samuel 75, 88, 94
Sadler's Wells 28
St. George Society 47
St. Patrick's Cathedral 42, 108 n127
St. Steven's Church 76
St. Thomas Episcopal Church 73, 76
Sandford, General 56, 57
Sans Souci 27, 30, 31, 32, 65, 67
Schiefflin, Richard L. 77
Schmidt, M. 54
Seaman, Henry 73
Sefton, John 48, 56, 62
Sir Henry (horse) 22
Sloat, Martha and John 84
Snook, John 63
"Sociable" 24, 25
Society for the Encouragement of Faithful Domestic Servants 72
Sontag, Henrietta 69
Southard, Samuel Lewis 75, 76
Sperry's Garden 26 fig., 28
Spring Gardens 27–28
Sproull, Thomas 53
Steele, John 46
Stewart, A. T. 44, 71, 97, 102 n29, 110 n145
Stourenel, Joseph 90
Stretton, George 67

Strong, George Templeton 76, 97, 107 n102, 108 n126
Sylvester, Mary 12, 93, 94, 95
Tappan, Arthur 72
Toby Philpot's 44
Tompkins, Col. William 42
Tontine, The 16
Trinity Church 16, 74, 75
Tripler Hall 65
Union Garden 29
Van Rensselaer, P. S. 63
Van Rensselaer, J. Rutsen Jr. 76
Van Rensselear, Mrs. J. 77
Van Rensselaer, Stephen III 27, 32, 52, 92
Vauxhall Garden 28, 29, 34
Victoria, Queen 47
Wainwright, John 67
Wainwright, Rev. Jonathan M. 76
Walker, Rev. William D. 95
Wallach, James Sr. 48, 48 fig., 64
Walmsley, Jane 85–86, 87 fig.
Washburn, Rector Edward 94
Washington Gardens 29
Washington, George 39
Washington Hall 44
Washington Hotel 36
Watson, John Fanning 41
Watson, Selina 40–41
Watts, J. 87
Webb, James Watson 75
Weir, Silas 88
Welch, General 65
Wheatley, William 48, 97
Whelpley, Rev. Phillip Melancthon 15
Wood, Henry 64
Wood, Mayor Fernando 69
Woodhull, Mayor 56
"You Naughty, Naughty Men" 96
Young Men's Christian Association 87, 95–96

*Set in Bulmer types.
Designed by Jerry Kelly,
New York.*

CPSIA information can be obtained
at www.ICGtesting.com
Printed in the USA
BVHW01s0153110718
521088BV00022B/49/P